THE TIE THAT BINDS

The
TIE
That
BINDS

*A COLLECTION OF WRITINGS
ABOUT FATHERS & DAUGHTERS,
MOTHERS & SONS*

Edited by Sandra Martz

Papier-Mache Press
Watsonville, California

Second Edition

ISBN: 0-918949-19-X Paperback
      0-918949-20-3 Hardcover

Editorial assistance: Bobbie Goodwin and Lee Rathbone
Production assistance: Chris Ballin and Roberta Shepherd
Typography: Elizabeth Turner

Grateful acknowledgement is made to the following publications which first published some of the material in this book: *From Redwing: Voices of a Hundred Years Ago* (Foothills Publishing) for "Heather Smith" by Katharyn Machan Aal; *Laws of the Land* for "Mushrooms," © 1981 by David Baker, Ahsahta/Boise State University; *Crucible*, Spring 1988 for "My Son at the Wheel" by Mary Balazs; *The Detroit Free Press, Detroit Magazine*, September 18, 1983, for "A Man of Many Hats" by Therese Becker; *Family & Other Strangers* (Word Works Inc.) for "Conversation with a Son," © by Shirley G. Cochrane; *The MacGuffin* 4.1 (Spring 1987):88-91 for "Optical Illusion" by Maxine Combs; *Toyon, The Literary Journal of Humboldt State University*, 1988, for "The Ice Man Still Comes" by Peter Coyne; *Bringing Home Breakfast* (Black Willow Press) for "Jennifer, Reading" by Mark DeFoe; *Cimarron Review* for "Tennis Lessons" by Emilio DeGrazia; *Negative Capability* 3:1-2, for "Summer Custody" by Pamela Ditchoff; *Kindred Spirit* for "Weekend Visit" by Sue Saniel Elkind; "On Being a Father" (Seasonings Press) for "Gathering Chestnuts" by Michael S. Glaser; *New York Times* for "Empty" by Ursula Hegi; *The Village* (Dolphin-Moon Press) for "At the Dancing School of the Sisters Schwarz" by Judson Jerome; *Wormwood Review* (Mag Press) and *POOP and other poems* (Maelstrom Press) for "poop," © 1972 by Gerald Locklin; *Notice Me!* (Sunflower Ink) for "Ellen" and "A Tar Baby" by Ric Masten; *Bay Leaves*, 1984-1985, (Copple House Books, Inc.) for "In My Father's Fields" by Nancy Frost Rouse, © 1986 by The Poetry Council of N.C., Inc.; *La Bella Figura*, Summer 1988, n.2, for "My Papa Mostly with a Needle" by Savina A. Roxas; *Stalking the Florida Panther* (Word Works, Inc.) for "To Fish, to Remember" by Enid Shomer; *The Greenfield Review*, Spring 1976, 5:1-2, and *Question and Form in Literature* (Scott Foresman & Co.) for "heritage" by Anita Skeen; *The Florida Review*, 13:2, 1985, for "The Light" by Floyd Skloot; *Southern Poetry Review*, Fall 1979 for "My Daughter Considers Her Body" by Floyd Skloot; *Loonfeather*, Spring 1987, 8:1, for "Lightning" by Randeane Tetu; *West Branch*, n.17, © 1985 for "Someone Could Do That" by Donna Trussell.

THE TIE THAT BINDS

Contents

Fathers & Daughters

Mothers & Sons

Preface

As an editor of anthologies I am always searching for new themes —subjects deep enough to inspire passion in the writers and complex enough to provoke different perspectives in the stories and poems. Taking a cue from the writer's credo—write about what you know—I was inspired by my experiences with my father and my two sons to pull together material that would focus on the special bonds that develop between opposite sex parents and children—those emotional ties that bind fathers and daughters, mothers and sons.

The poems, stories, and photographs selected for the anthology came from a diverse group of men and women: students and teachers, filmmakers and social workers, librarians and dancers, housewives and housepainters. A few of the contributors are full-time writers or photographers but for most producing creative works is an act of love.

When written from the perspective of mothers or fathers, the material in this collection is more likely to explore the early years, the joy of being a new parent, the excitement and anxiety of watching children grow up and go out on their own. Daughters and sons, however, more often deal with midlife years and unresolved conflicts, aging parents and role reversals.

In putting together the collection I found that my own experiences were often mirrored in the poems and stories. It has often been difficult for me to articulate my feelings about those experiences and so I dedicate this book—to my father George, "God of that untidy underworld, wizard of tools," in faith that we will always find the words we need to say before "that fragile life strand" breaks; to my son John, in gratitude for he who "brings me seasoned wood on winter's coldest day" and whose fire "burns on long after he has gone"; and to my son, James, "child with dark November eyes" in faith that "Something I need to know is here—an alchemy we will work together." Blest be the Ties That Bind.

Fathers
&
Daughters

Small Song for Daddy

W.D. Ehrhart

It isn't like my daughter
to awaken at one a.m.—
but here she is
wide-eyed and smiling.

I lift her to my lap
where she sits uncomplaining
as my arms encircle her.

She pulls the hairs on my chest
idly, wiggles her toes, sighs
almost as if in meditation,
and begins to sing softly,

the language hers alone,
the voice clear and fragile
as water striking stone.

New in a world where new
is all she knows, she sings
for each new wonder
she discovers—as if those

curtains, the chair, that
box of Kleenex were created
solely to delight her.

And they do. And she sings,
not knowing she is singing
for a father much in need
of her particular song.

Phillip Shelton

Jennifer, Reading

Mark DeFoe

In a cone of lamplight my daughter
sits reading—or pretending she can.
She pulls words from pictures, floats her voice
up, lilting the sounds like clear crystal
bubbles popping above the sofa.

Her small voice bears my intonations—
father and teacher and oracle.
Yet the more she reads, the more it fades—
"Doctor Tonsils has a lion in his bathtub."
"The princess has a sister who is weird."
"Oh, Woodshopper, what fangs your mother has."

And when she reaches the story's end
her lips press together in a prim
satisfaction. The sheen on her
brown hair glows in the light. She looks up
into my eyes, not too proud, but pleased
that she has set things right at last.
In her story we all got a doll,
a painless rabies shot, a Big Mac,
and at least a chance at revenge.

Louise M. Kirst-Gesch

poop

Gerald Locklin

my daughter, blake, is in kindergarten. they are teaching her to be
   a docile citizen and, incidentally to read. concurrently, like
   many of us, she has become a trifle anal compulsive. complica-
   tions ensue.

i ask her what she has learned today. she says, "i learned the
   pledge of allegiance." "how does it go?" i ask. "it goes," she
   says, "i poop allegiance to the poop of the united poops of
   ameripoop."

"that's good," i say, "that's very good. what else?" "o say can you
   poop, by the dawn's early poop, what so proudly we
   pooped . . ."

for christmas, she improvises, "away in a pooper, all covered with
   poop, the little lord poopus lay pooping his poop."

she has personalized other traditional favorites as well. someone,
   perhaps her grandmother, tried to teach her the "our father."
   her version goes, "our pooper, who art in poopland, hallowed
   be thy poop. thy poopdom poop, thy poop be pooped, on earth
   as it is in poopland."

surely hemingway would feel one-upped. surely the second
   pooping is at hand.

a fortune teller told us blake would be our greatest sorrow and
   our greatest joy. already, it is true.

Phillip Shelton

Gathering Chestnuts

Michael S. Glaser

When chestnuts fall, their pods open
to heart and egg-shaped gems—nuts smooth
and shiny, with leathery skin.

Come Christmas, we will roast them, but for now
they are gathered as best we can. We sit
at the kitchen table. While I slice vegetables

for dinner, my daughter examines each chestnut,
putting these into egg cartons, placing those
back in their pods like puzzle pieces

before taking them out again, rearranging them,
feeling their smooth skin, turning them over
and over until she seems to know for certain

just where each should go. I marvel at her
strategies—how her tiny fingers release
each from its shell, determine for each

its place with such confident grace, such
grown-up busy-ness, absorbed in detail
and task. We talk and work until our thoughts

take us away in the silence of hands moving.
And when I look again her way, I see her
facing me like a mirror, her elbow propped

on the table, like mine, her arm curved
into a question mark, her small hand,
a loose-fisted rest for her head. She grins

Chris Bartlett

and I smile back, seeing myself reflected
in her brown, chestnut eyes, imagining she sees
herself, for this unguarded instant, in mine.

The Light

Floyd Skloot

At five by nightlight I stood in the hall
where a buzzing had led me from a dream
of dancing circles in air. In the fall
chill I wished I'd put on my wife's old cream

colored robe tossed aside with last night's love.
I'd grown used to the streetlight's steady drone,
but this was a new noise, harsher, less of
a swarm than a nectar-drunk bee alone

above clover. Outside my daughter's room
I heard wings. Her bed was empty, blanket
deflated, stuffed bears strewn. But in the gloom
I saw her feet jutting from the closet

where she'd moved to sleep. A fluorescent light
hummed in her hive. The book spread on her chest
like a comforter held the restless night
off as I hovered in the doorway, dressed

in nothing but skin, trapped in the spaces
between her breaths. When she was an infant,
I cooked rice cereal mixed with traces
of yogurt and wheat germ, a breakfast meant

to be as rich as royal jelly. She
refused to eat it, seeking nourishment
instead from a fistful of dry honey
covered Cheerios. Now I pause, intent

on the throb in her throat given voice by
the light, no more understanding her new
impulses than the beekeeper knows why
workers choose to build queen cells when they do.

Ellen

Ric Masten

my youngest daughter
likes to ride
to the mailbox with me

she fetches the mail
while i turn the car around
then she climbs into the back seat

and doles out my letters
slowly
inspecting each envelope

till i am infuriated
and turn red
and shout at her

Ellen!
gimme
the letters!

my youngest daughter likes to do this
it is one of the few times
she has my full attention

A Couple of Loose Nuts

James Bogan

> *We weren't very tired*
> *but we were very merry*
> *As we rode back & forth*
> *on the Wheatland Ferry.*

Blue-eyed Anna is like a lot of seven-year-old girls. For instance, when I suggested we take off on an adventure instead of going to school, she immediately said, "Yes!" We did not know what was going to happen or where, but it did by the time we meandered our way to the Wheatland Ferry which crosses the Willamette River north of Salem. We left the car on shore and walked aboard because, as the captain told us, "Pedestrians ride for free."

The Willamette is swift flowing and brown-broad on this afternoon verging into evening. A ferry has plied this crossing for seventy-five years and the current model, *The Matheney,* is like a miniature aircraft carrier whose deck can accommodate six cars or one garbage truck. The craft, powered by an electric motor, is kept from being pushed downstream by a cable that tethers it to a horizontal course across the river. Anna gazes with curiosity at the turbulent water that billows against the side of the boat. Me, too, until the honking of a dozen geese in a grayed vee overhead draws my attention into the clouds.

When we reach the other side, the tongue of the deck fits to the road. The captain drops the chain stretched in front of the cars by throwing a lever in his cabin. The cars drive off, one scraping its muffler as it lurches from flat deck to the angled road. Two pickups are waiting to make the return trip. My eyes cannot get enough of the river swirling with eddies. Anna jumps up into my arms to get a better view. When we get back to where we started, she says, "One more time?" Sure.

And we set off again. This time a gawky heron flies by, trailing its long legs.

And another return. "One more time, please?" Sure.

The sun's lessening light reflects the brown river red.

And return. "One more time, please, please?" Are you sure? So sure she grabs the rail with both hands, catching me in the inescapable trap of a seven-year-old's simple desire. But the captain will think we are a couple of nuts! And she replies rather confidentially, "Well, Daddy, you know we are."

The last round trip is the best. Douglas firs are silhouetted on the far bank against a dim sky. The river sounds augment in the darkness and our own laughter joins the night: "Eight rides on the Wheatland Ferry and pedestrians ride for free. Hee, hee, hee." The Manhattan skyline viewed from the Staten Island Ferry is a lot brighter than this dark Oregon tree line, but look out, that voyage will set you back two bits.

At the Dancing School
of the Sisters Schwarz

Judson Jerome

Silently grave as voyeurs in a powder room,
we fathers sit with coats folded on knees
this visiting day, watching Miss Hermene
teach fourteen girls the elements of ballet.

Accompaniment is struck in chords upon
the Steinway grand. Outside a siren grieves:
law for a speeder below. Miss Hermene slaps
time on her thighs, her words exact and low.

Her muscular, liquid arms demonstrate grace
to daughters in pink tights along the *barre.*
Battement tendu! and fourteen arches curve.
She spots a limp leg, squats for a better view,

then sweeps from child to child, chin high, commanding—
love in her old eyes, discipline on her tongue,
correct as a queen, and fierce beneath her charm.
Our girls come hushed and quick, hair back, nails clean;

chubby or bony, concave or convex of chest,
gangly, petite or tough, their slippers whisper
in the studio. No scratching or wiggling now,
but each projects life to her pointed toe.

My own, the smallest, still sticks out her tummy,
curving her limber spine. Her feet are flat,
her limbs thin. Braids swing as she takes correction
like kisses—with freckly cheeks and toothy grin.

Phillip Shelton

Material comes raw, but Miss Hermene
makes girlflesh pirouette and count strict time.
Covertly I squirm—loosely sitting, like nature,
thinking how daffodils look to a worm.

Glissez! Sautez! Pliez! Knees skinned at skating
now bend in diamond shapes around the room,
and fathers dream of the stage where ballerinas
are purer than people, selfless, without age,

and Miss Hermene in her Ohio winter
dreams rigorous designs for the new day
and tender swarm: the power of grace, the truth
of timing, the immortality of form.

My Daughter Considers Her Body

Floyd Skloot

She examines her hand, fingers spread wide.
Seated, she bends over her crossed legs
to search for specks or scars and cannot hide
her awe when any mark is found. She begs
me to look, twisting before her mirror,
at some tiny bruise on her hucklebone.
Barely awake, she studies creases her
arm developed as she slept. She has grown
entranced with blemish, begun to know
her body's facility for being
flawed. She does not trust its will to grow
whole again, but may learn that too, freeing
herself to accept the body's deep thirst
for risk. Learning to touch her wounds comes first.

She Slips Away

Lowell Jaeger

Every other weekend with you, my daughter,
we practiced what was ours
to hold onto, and what was out of our hands.
Jacks, or tag. Or when the musk of wet maples
bundled us into my camper—sacks of pajamas,
socks, envelopes of loose news from your school—
I wanted to grab the sky blue afternoon,
out where the golden leaves unlatched
themselves, effortless as your world should be.

But rain. Sleet. And as we bumped along
the grade to camp, early scraps of snow.
That night with hot chocolate we huddled,
picking on chips, dull sausage, dealing
long rounds of Old Maid. Under faded
lantern fire, brave flickers of your smile.
Let it go, I whispered to no one as I rolled out
your blankets, thinking how you won't take my hand
anymore in shopping malls or crossing streets.

Before breakfast you were outside bending your kite
frame, my old red shirt spliced for a tail.
Snow vanished, sky full of violent gray; high
knoll of corn stubble waiting for us to climb.
How—just as the kite was lifting—how
did it slip away? One moment your laughter
buoyed me, next I'm leaping furrows, bounding after
a runaway bobbin of string, till I drop my reach,
and I know by my pounding heart why you won't take
my hand.
      By the time I turn back, there's a hundred

yards between us from where you stand
your broken ground. You stare up at your kite
trailing off into the great gray dome. Fists
curled in your sweater pockets, and you won't cry.

To Fish, to Remember

Enid Shomer

Daddy is with me here on the pier
at Cedar Key. The fish strung by their gills,
the shower of water from the bait bucket
bring him back. Night fishing
from Biscayne Bridge. I'm six,
chewed by mosquitoes, sticky with cocoa butter.

Again and again his spinning reel unzips
the black water. He is never pleased,
except by a record haul.
We are the baggage he drags along,
my mother pretending interest
in chum, swivels and lures.

I don't want to fish. I want to comb
the Saran hair of my Toni doll,
cuddle her as if I know how it's done.
I am made to stand on the bridge quietly
so as not to scare them away
from the king of fish, the king

of the sport of kings, the king
of ulcers. He needed silence
when we ate, silence when we fished
and the anonymous roar of the track
where he gambled away two businesses.
For years I took his angry looks

for love. For years I avoided water.
Now I bait my hook as he taught me,
pleating the shrimp to conceal the barbs.

I try to forgive him with each fish
I catch, but every time it's myself
I see on the end of the line—
struggling silently,
intimate with the hook.

Lightning

Randeane Tetu

"Sixth grader now," Uncle Harry said when they got out of the car at the lake. "How does it feel?"

"Well, I'm not a sixth grader until September," Tina said.

"Oh, yes. As soon as you stop being a fifth grader, you start being a sixth grader."

Tina went around to the trunk of the car, stepping on the brown pine needles and the sand. She thought there was something she had to learn before sixth grade. She took the suitcase her mother handed her and followed her to the cottage. Aunt Laureen already had supper ready and her father asked about the canoe. "It's down at the dock," Uncle Harry said. "You can take it out after supper, but it's supposed to thunderstorm."

Tina knew they wouldn't get back tonight. A thunderstorm was coming. The air was full of its sweet pressure. The storm would come up over the trees at the end of the lake by the spillway and crash over the lake and the cottages. The thrilling goose pimples stood up on her arms.

Uncle Harry had said, "Don't be out on the water if it storms."

"Why?" she said.

She would keep her eye out for little coves with sandy beaches. They would pull ashore and camp overnight.

"Because lightning is seeking the highest point. And on a flat lake that would be you." The shiver zipped down the front of her.

Then they climbed down from the dock into the polished wood inside the canoe. She put up the backrest as he showed her. She sat in the front and her Dad got down off the dock behind her. The canoe rocked and settled into the water. Uncle Harry pushed them off.

Her paddle seemed heavy to hold up, but against the water it seemed light. Her force, puny against the water. Where she pushed she made a tiny pointed dent at the near blade of the paddle and the lake filled it right in. No one would have known she'd been there.

Sandra Gregory

The canoe didn't move. She switched the paddle to the other side and pushed, and the paddle skimmed across the water and flung up against the side so she just caught the end again before it was out of her grasp.

Then Daddy put in his paddle. He was wearing a white tee shirt and swimming trunks. His legs looked very white, but she couldn't see him. He pushed against the water and the canoe moved. It surged at first and then again, and then it started going smoothly. The lake was just outside the canoe, the wood holding it from touching her feet, her lap.

The lake was smooth, pressed down by the heavy air, and still, so the bird songs glided across it, skimmed across like flat stones skipped off it.

"Just paddle one side," Daddy said. "I'll change sides and steer us."

She put the paddle in again and now that they were moving she could push against the water that was already going in the right direction. Her strokes were too deep and got stuck. She tried them higher and they skimmed and she had to catch the end of the paddle and Daddy kept pushing the canoe from behind.

Then she got the depth and filled the paddle each time and pushed. Sunlight glinted in the little eddies she made with the paddle and colors formed like oil on puddles. When she looked up, they were going across the lake to the wooded shore.

She didn't look behind her. The canoe wasn't on top of the water, but sunken into it and keeping the water out. They went past the water that was in front of them, and it went behind them, but it didn't look as if they were moving.

Sunlight shone up the tree trunks and bushes on the other side. The light looked as if it were shining up instead of down and the leaves made shadows on the leaves above them instead of on the leaves below. They looked yellow and gold and warm instead of green.

Then they were closer and she could see that the bushes were blueberry bushes. Down toward the spillway, clouds climbed up, but the sun came in from the other side and lit up the bushes and the lake. Then suddenly she could see the bottom. She looked into the lake and could see stones covered with dust or whatever dust would be underwater, fuzzy and brown. Daddy turned the canoe to go along shore.

She didn't know what it would be that she should learn this summer. Ronnie had stood in front of her in line and reached back and pushed her skirt in between her legs. But Jack Raymond had tucked his hand into her skirt from the back when they were washing paint dishes in the janitor's closet. If Ronnie or Jackie had been in the canoe she would not have wanted to stay overnight.

It didn't look like lightning yet but she watched along the shore for a place they could stop if it started. They could build a fire and eat blueberries.

Daddy stopped pushing and pulled the paddle across his knees. Water ran from the blade into the lake, and she pulled in her paddle. He lit a cigarette, and the boat drifted toward the light on the water. The smell of the match and the smell of the cigarette smoke came around the canoe. She didn't look toward the other shore where the cottages were.

If they spent the night here, Daddy could light a fire and smoke cigarettes. They would turn the canoe up and prop it to make a shelter, and they would be dry while all around them would be gentle wet. Soft wet, not the glazing wet and trample of a heavy storm. Just the fuzzy wet that made being dry and warm feel like something special.

At the cottage they might worry a little. It would be good if they worried a little because then Mom would feel sorry she had scolded about the sugar on the floor and hollered about ants. The linoleum right there was always sandy from their feet anyway. In the cottage they would be drinking coffee and saying, "Hope it doesn't storm."

Uncle Harry and Aunt Laureen would walk outside down under the trees as they did last year and come in later and say, "Too many mosquitoes." Her mother would look across the lake and start to wonder where they were and start to be sorry about the sugar she'd spilled.

That would be tonight and in the morning she'd be waking up under the canoe and the sun would be out and the birds would be going crazy calling across the trees. And the ground would smell like summer and the inside of the canoe.

Something in Mom's and Dad's room didn't smell like either of them. When she used to be frightened in the night and go in there to sleep, Mom would let her in and say, "Lie still, now," and Tina would lie as still as she could until she had to turn over. Then Mom would say, "Lie still," and she would say, "I am," and move around to get comfortable. Then she would breathe with her mother. Try to take breaths as long as hers and when she woke up Daddy would be gone from bed and his slippers would be gone. And the whole time the bed would smell different than either of them. She wondered if she smelled different when she slept, but her bed smelled the same to her every night.

When Mom opened her scarf drawer, Tina could smell her perfume on the scarves, but Mom said she couldn't smell it any more so maybe that's what happened. Your own smell got lost on you, but other people could find it.

Her mother wouldn't let her put on any of her perfume because when she wore the same kind as Grandma, Daddy said, "Don't wear that. It smells like my mother." Tina didn't see why it made any difference since Daddy loved them all.

Daddy's cigarette hit the water next to where her paddle had been. The paper turned gray and the flecks of tobacco showed through.

"Head home?" Daddy said. "Hold your paddle on that side. Just hold it still and I'll turn us."

Light had faded off the surface and dark was gathering as the dust had gathered on the underwater rocks, coming together on the bottom like "mother" in the bottom of the bottles of cider getting hard in their cellar.

Tina thought one of them must have the wrong information, but she didn't know which one. Ronnie had an older brother that everyone called Lover so she supposed he had it right. But then, Ronnie wasn't too smart in school so she couldn't count on it. Anyway she didn't stand near him in line and she only washed paint dishes if one of the girls was going to.

All the girls brought in lilac blossoms and carried them around the playground. The girls played wedding. The boys came over to their side of the playground, but the girls wouldn't let them play because they snickered when they were supposed to say, "I do." Ronnie came to the girls' side and said, "I do, but don't tell my mother," and the boys hooted and rushed him back to their own side.

In sixth grade all the girls carried pocketbooks with a hairbrush and pens in them. She already knew she couldn't wear nylons but she thought maybe she could carry a pocketbook.

From behind her, her father said, "You're growing up, honey." He spoke the words outside as if he'd been carrying them inside and turning them around with the cigarette smoke. He spoke the words carefully, not in his usual voice. And she had the quick catch of noticing a heartbeat, thinking, "Here comes something." It was dark and she didn't turn around. "You've heard the kids talking about boys and girls. You're growing up, but you're still a little girl. You'll have plenty of time for boys when you're older." She thought he would say more.

"I don't know what boys are like now but they're probably the same as they were when I was in sixth grade at Beck School, and when I was in sixth grade we used to try to get a girl pressed into a corner so we could feel her up a little. Not to hurt her. I'm not trying to scare you."

Her paddle was trailing in the water and she pulled it out.

"But if anybody tries touching you, don't be afraid to give him a good punch or a mean kick. Better if you don't get in a corner to start with."

His words fell into the water around her. She wanted them back a moment longer to be sure she had them right, that she hadn't missed something. But they'd gone down to the bottom with the fuzz.

She wanted to say, What is it you think I already know? but they were headed toward the cottage. Maybe if they had stayed on the wooded shore.

It had taken no time to cross the lake. They were coming in to the dock, the cottage getting bigger and stepping up higher on the slope.

Daddy held the canoe in with his paddle and then pulled them close with his hand. He climbed onto the dock and held the canoe for her. She wouldn't look at him. With one foot on the dock, stretching up, her other foot pushed the canoe away from the dock. The canoe skidded out and she stepped into the water, bobbed up and under before he caught her and lifted her up. "There, Baby."

In the night she woke and heard the storm. Trees lashed outside the window and lightning tore down the night. Too late, she thought, way too late, and fell asleep again and dreamed of lightning creeping over the hills and looking over spillways for the highest point.

My Papa Mostly with a Needle

Savina A. Roxas

My papa mostly with a needle
sewed custom-made coats for
Fifth Avenue stores, blue-serge
skirts to go with my middy blouses,
knickers for Frank, Mike, Bon
and Peter, curtains for the back
windows that faced the court;

used black roasted coffee
hand ground in the mill
mounted on the kitchen wall
for our after dinner espresso
called Mediterranean mud
by the kids next door;

played Rosa Ponselle's
opera records and "Hard Hearted Hannah
the Vamp of Savannah"
on the windup Victrola;

told us Giotto never forgot
his humble beginnings,
faith could move mountains
if we helped push, and that
dressing well and speaking well
made us anybody's equal.

Les Miserables

Barbara Goldberg

"They make the hero handsome
to pervert the minds of children."

Ten years old, sassy, and just beginning
to doubt God, when my father took me
to a movie about a poor man who stole
a loaf of bread for his wife and infant.
It was an old film, grainy and blurred
as the boundary between right and wrong.
Later I said I pitied the man, already
a little in love with his pompadour
and animal grace. "Stealing? You approve
of stealing?" my father's look branding me
as criminal. "But they were starving!"
I cried. "That's decadence masquerading
as compassion." He saw through my desire
for a father as handsome, as corruptible.
I persisted, until my father reached out
and struck me twice across the face,
so scrupulous his devotion to the law
he renounced the passion of a young girl.

Lori Burkhalter-Lackey

The Carpenter's Daughter

Catherine Shaw

. . . watched her father
wield the saw,
sand the wood.
She'd crouch close
as planks were split,
press nose to teak,
tweak pine's knots,
bold against splinters!
Down canted stairs
she'd run
to where a wild dust
fogged the air,
and wires wormed,
and boards
were everywhere.
God of that untidy
underworld,
wizard of tools,
how I loved to watch you work!
Your wide hands:
so precise.
Your concentrating eyes:
so piercing clear.
"See: a delicate
mechanism," you'd say,
pointing out
some gear or power tooth,
holding up
some new infatuation.
In deference
to its elegance

you stayed sober,
as if escorting
a fine woman.
In deference
to your reverence,
at your side
I stayed as quiet
as the wood.

In the Country

Lynn Lauber

Because I was so young when he died, I hardly knew my father's father, August. He died in the country, in the same abrupt manner as he'd lived—simply closed his eyes one morning and let his old heart stop. But I had a late view of him, according to my mother, who had taken, along with my father's name, a proprietary interest in the Dardios, as if somehow through marriage they were more hers than his. This did not mean she loved them, as much as she thought she knew them, and in her middle years, when she had run out of toddlers to thwart and part-time jobs that drained off like cream the top layer of her nervous energy, she took to researching my father's family tree in great detail. She became his archivist, in a way.

It was not an enterprise for which I could muster much enthusiasm, mostly because the women on these diagrammed sheets only seemed to have been born, married, and died. Sometimes their maiden names were lost for good, but this did not seem to bother my mother, who charted the endeavors of the lost men in my father's family with a zeal I found suspicious.

She had her own family, of course, who were less scattered and whom we saw more often, but she was as curiously detached from them as I would be at the family gatherings she later orchestrated.

"Nothing's ever new here," she sighed as she sat apart at barbecues and birthdays, listlessly eating the three-bean salads and Jell-O molds that constituted the extent of her own culinary imagination. She seemed to be implying that if it weren't for bonds of blood, she would never have chosen to know these people—her family—at all.

I didn't think she would have chosen my father's family either, but she had certainly chosen my father, with his background of thrift and silence. There were so many siblings, mostly sisters, on his side of the family and a number had died long ago, some through difficult-sounding illnesses, like diphtheria, others by that most trying act of all — being born. My father's remaining sisters had been scattered through marriage by the time I could know them, in regions of the country I could not even locate on a map. And when they did show up yearly at family reunions, in tandem with their husbands, who were in the Navy or held vague jobs at National Cash Register or GE, they were so reduced by marriage and motherhood, so sunken into themselves, that I could hardly locate the family features that stood out so distinctly in the few sepia photographs my mother had gathered of my father's family.

My father was a struggling insurance salesman for Mutual of Omaha by the time his father died and seemed curiously detached from any roots other than the rather shallow ones we were all feebly putting down right then.

"He doesn't have time for things like that," my mother said, reporting on him as if we weren't all living together in the same house.

I could see for myself how the world of business, the nights of adding machines and cigarettes, the jostling for accounts, all in the rather shameful pursuit of insurance—which involved, as far as I could tell, scaring the wits out of people about what would happen after they died—was taking an extraordinary toll on my father, who seemed just barely himself. Even on Saturdays, after his breakfast of glazed doughnuts, he went immediately to the Elks for poker, as if he could not bear for a moment to be without the company of men, amidst the air of futile competition.

When we had him was on days like this one: a Sunday, when my mother manages to intimidate us all into attending church, although once there, her mind is more on the upcoming dinner than the words of warning and doom which register plainly on my father and settle into me slowly, like some time-released drug all through the day.

We have him for our heavy Sunday meal, which has simmered on low throughout the services, the entire dinner in a black speckled roaster, so that the roast beef and carrots and potatoes cook into each other in a disconcerting way and look exhausted, defeated, by the time they reach our plates. Having overeaten, my father snores in front of the dreadful shows that air on Sunday afternoon TV, shows that seem to be gathered together as some sort of punishment for our expecting entertainment on a holy day. I lie on the floor in front of my darning mother while we watch Oral Roberts cry over the blind and lame and hearing disabled, clucking with her skeptically when hearing aids and crutches are thrown through the air, as he cries, "Thank Jesus! You're saved." We watch *Industry on Parade*, a great dull program that takes you inside automated dairy plants and steel foundries, showing a dark, mechanized world that you don't really want to know about. This is followed, just as my father is about to wake, with *High School Quiz*, where genius boys from Indiana instantly provide physics and astronomy answers that none of us will know, ever.

I am more disconcerted on these flat Sunday afternoons by this show than any of the others. I want to be quick and full of numbers; if not, I want at least to be active, not lying about in a great herd with my family. My mother, by this third hour of television, has put down her darning and is watching my father doze in a way that is as beseeching as it is critical.

"He's getting to be just like his father," she says in the explanatory voice that guides use when describing inanimate objects in museums, just before she wakes him with "Robert, come on. It's time to take us for a ride."

This seems to be our due, this Sunday afternoon ride, which my father has to preside over, although my mother has a perfectly valid Ohio driver's license in her neat billfold and can take the two of us anywhere we want with perfect legality and ease. But we wait for him, emerging from sleep with a boyish look that disappears when reality — this waning Sunday, my mother's expectant face, the world of work and worry ahead of him — finally rises up again in his consciousness. But even seeing all this, he says, "Okay."

We never drive anywhere new on these rides, just out of town via back roads that cut across soybean and corn fields, past a creek we fished in long ago when my father still had time. My father's in a good mood once we reach the country and honks at any lone man we see. "Hey there, Charlie!" he calls out and the man always waves back. This anonymous greeting, based on nothing, thrills me, as if there is a great goodwill out in the world, waiting to be tapped, as if anyone we want to know is just there, ready for us, only needing to be honked to, waved at.

During this ride, as on many others when my mother is tired or silent, memories of childhood dribble from my father, as if he is releasing a too-hot drink. He especially talks about his mother, perhaps because she died first and suffered most; her crowning pain was the amputation of her legs the year before she died. "Even then she maneuvered around on some wheeled contraption to mop the floors," my father says. What she did without, the deaths of children she endured without complaint —she seems mythical, saintly even in her silent strength—and as my father talks, he lets the car veer to the median in the sorrow of remembering her. This is enough to jolt my mother out of her reverie and she navigates him back into the safety of the suburbs, to streets where she can note curtains and lawn furniture and petunia arrangements that she might mimic later on. And just as surely she steers his memories toward the men of his family, those traveling begetters whose lives she has so charted on her tree, saying, "Why don't you tell Laura that story about your old Uncle Jake."

And my father does and I listen, as we let her take us back to our world, away from what we are drawn to and scared of—that green region of feeling that opens up, like a silent lake, whenever we drive into the country.

Ritual Slaughter

Bina Goldfield

I pretended he was not my father
the first time I brought his lunch
to the kosher poultry store.
His place was in the back room
piled with crates of squawking chickens.
Swirls of feathers clogged the air,
gray wisps clung to his lashes.
He held a chicken close to his chest,
one hand arched the neck back, the other
slit the throat.

I pretended it was not a chicken
stuck upside down in a hole
on the tray, draining
red into a basin below,
its toes grasping air.

I pretended it was not the knife,
the one I watched him
dreamily hone every evening.

He pretended he did not know
each time I kissed him
I held my breath,
the smell of slaughter in his skin.

Chris Bartlett

You Can't Say "No" to Daddy

Nancy du Plessis

you can't say "no" to Daddy
not to the man who pays your rent
buys you butterscotch ice cream cones
and every pretty party dress
why little miss tease
you can't refuse a good provider
hankering for his honey child
but Daddy won't hurt
such a pearl of a girl
and no one will ever know
of these real fine times   see
cause Papa just said so   and
you don't resist Big Daddy Dear
no his own special sweetie's
a snug tight squeeze
and he's flying so fast—oh!
Daddy loves his baby darling
who sure satisfies her old man
who always gets it all his way
cause you can't ever
say "no" to Daddy

Torn Pictures

Patti Tana

I have not seen him since I was ten
but remember his face was big
with stubbled cheeks. Thick hairs
poked from his nostrils.
Starting to bald, he'd comb the remaining strands
back over the space. I don't remember his eyes
or his smile, only his angry stare
and spit through clenched teeth
as he struck me.

I remember too the smell of house paint
he let me scratch off his face
in a moment of gentle holding.
But usually he smelled stale
from cigarettes and whiskey.   Years later
when I would kiss a boy through fumes
of alcohol and tobacco, I would
think of my father.

When I looked through my mother's
yellowed photographs, I found only
torn pictures—
ragged edges where he should have been.

Incantation

Dori Appel

Father, bring
your good green tool box,
since you left
the house in great disrepair—
at every seam the glue's unstuck
bolts fly from unhinged doors
things squeak
and all our griefs
are spilling on the floor.

In the yard
your children shove
each other's heads
through croquet wickets,
while upstairs mother knits
a great blue net.
Come quick, come quick!
For when she's done
she will hang herself up
like a fish in the marketplace,
while her gills slowly close
with spite.

Your green tool box
rests on the stone step out back,
recalling the magic
of your mended lamp cord,
the magic of your suspended shelf.
Come now my father wizard,
come from your placid spin
through winking stars

to this old leaning house.
Open the box
rattling prayers
of screws and bolts and washers,
and fix us up.

Humming "The Old Geezer"

Sally Croft

You're Protestant
and I'm not supposed to love you.
Aunt Margaret says
you're going straight to Hell.
Mama loved you
and God punished her.
That's why she died.

All of us have brown eyes.
Yours are blue.
And on Sunday morning
when the blue stained glass
flames above my head
it's as though you are
with me. Even the Priests
can't keep you away.

We always sit in the living room
when you visit,
you in the big chair,
Aunt Margaret and Granma Anna
on each end of the sofa,
me in Mama's chair.
Nobody touching.

Before Mama died
and you lived with us
you used to hold me
on your lap and sing
funny songs

Oh, there was an old geezer
and he had a wooden leg,
and he had no tobacco
no tobacco could he beg...

You smelled of tobacco
and spice shaving soap,
your heart
thumped deep in my ear
against your chest.

After you leave
I hurry to your chair
while it's still warm
and still smells
of tobacco and spice.
I hum "The Old Geezer"
to myself and crumble
loose shreds of tobacco
until Aunt Margaret
sweeps in and opens
all the windows
"to let in the fresh air."

Ceremony

Leonore Wilson

after my father

I can see him now cleaning the fish
at his basin of pale rock
and basalt in the crumbling wall
above the city, a primitive altar,
a modern Acropolis, where he could look down
and see the streets, the horse arena,
the outdoor theater, and across
to my mother's mountain facing his.
His back to me like a priest
at Latin mass, his head bent, meditating,
elbows lifting, hands lost in the gutting
stained with blood as the sunset grew
and took the sky on those hot August nights.
This was his ceremony, splitting
the catfish, bluegill, and trout;
their severed fins and heads lining
the rocky shelf. Marble eyes catching
the light like dark round jewels
on a chalice. I had been washed there, too,
in that hard bin, my body cramping down;
he'd squeeze me in, washing my wholeness
with soap, scrubbing the earth
from my scalp. My mother washed me
in her sink on the opposite ridge. I moved
between them in summer imagining
my body was a fish split. He handed her
the money and took me with my sack of clothes
and my limbs down her road's twisting shoulder
and up the steep drive of his. Late at night,
in my childhood, I was caught
in the current of their needs.

Growing Children

Ernest Marshall

Awakened to early light
By laughter
My daughter and Lisa
Getting ready for school.
We three meet in the kitchen
Me ragged-robed and bleary-eyed.
This they make a joke of.
There's no sugar for coffee.
We laugh about that too.
I hear them rap in her bedroom
While I sit alone
Sip my coffee
Listen as parents will.
I flinch into a frown
Hearing Lisa say
She's moving to Virginia.
My daughter is slow to make friends.
Lisa mentions a hangover,
Not having her math.
I used to worry about that too.
Looking out upon the sun-steeped yard
I recall the garden that used to be there
That required my concern.
It took a little time each day.
A few precautions against cutworms and weather
But mostly I just let it grow.

Granola Love

William Borden

The poet in the next room writes a poem
about my making granola and sending
it to you. The poem is about

nurturing—men, fathers, nurturing. She
has some of it right.
Mixing the oats, wheat, bran,

honey, in the huge bowl,
with the long wooden spoon,
turning the moist mixture in the oven,

carefully, to leave the lumps
you like to eat with your fingers—
turning frequently to prevent burning—

then packing in ziplocs (not
in the tins of her poem)—I thought
not about nurturing but

sadness, that you were not here,
and wouldn't be, ever again, for long,
now that you're in college,

now that you're in love,
now that you will not need
these sweet baked flakes of pain

for what I am willing to feel
so that your leaving
will be noticed.

Tennis Lessons

Emilio De Grazia

When your life was too small
To cast a shadow halfway up my leg,
We did no more than chase the crazy ball.
Spindle-legged like a one-day fawn,
You sat on the concrete and wept.
Once you blasted the ball over the fence,
Commanded me to retrieve it like a bone:
A shameless power play.

In time you began to respect control.
Though mainly content to skitter, flail away,
You began to feel the ball's perfect pitch,
Bird released from its cage.
It was Shakespeare and Mozart in the round.
By then you were eager to guide
No less than the earth with your hands,
Hide that green apple behind your back,
Dare me to steal it from you.

Tomorrow, with the score forever tied
Love-love, we will spend sunsets gliding
That ball back and forth, back and fortn,
Your touch, graced by strong form,
Keeping the play just
Within my failing reach.

10-K

Darien Andreu

Jenny stood, crossed her legs, leaned over and reached for her shoes, but a tightness in her calves stopped her. She had to be satisfied with grabbing her ankles and pulling, two, three, four. Jenny stood, uncrossed and recrossed her legs, and once more turned herself into a hairpin. She looked past her knees and saw she was surrounded by running shoes, racing flats, and K-Mart specials. Some shoes bounced up and down in place, other pairs ran briskly across recently poured blacktop, all of them defied gravity from her upside down point of view. Pretty good turnout today. She stood, wobbling, as the blood drained from her head.

"Jenny!"

"Yeah?"

Jenny squinted, trying to tell from what part of the crowd her dad's voice had come.

Standing near the registration tent were many of the track club members. Looking tan and cheerful, they talked and stretched while waiting in line to register for their couples-age categories. They were a sharp contrast to the runners alternately jogging and sprinting around the perimeter of the starting area. Thin-muscled and pale, these runners, mostly young men, had done a good job of avoiding the Florida sun that sapped strength for fast workouts. A young woman's ponytail bobbed among them.

"Jenny!"

"Over here," she called.

Jenny's father ran toward her, down the road, beyond the starting line where the cars had pulled off in the dirt to park. His shirt shifted loosely over his shoulders, less loosely around his belly.

Short of breath, he handed Jenny her race number. "I've got us checked in," he said. "Your mother's back getting the camera out of the car."

Jenny smoothed her paper number. Her father held at least a dozen silver safety pins. "Think that's enough?" she asked. Her father continued to count.

Lori Burkhalter-Lackey

"Now, do you have four?" He put a number of pins in her hand.

Jenny counted. "Yep, got four." Her dad fumbled with his pins and crinkled number. "Here, let me help you pin that on," she said.

"No, no." He frowned and waved her away. "Go get your warm-up in. I'll have your mother help me with this."

"But you run first."

He waved her away. "Go on now. They'll be starting here soon."

Jenny jogged down the road, stopped, and glanced back. Her father's brows were drawn together; he was intent on pinning the race number to the front of his T-shirt. He jabbed, frowned, decided that the race number was crooked, and jabbed again. This wasn't like him. Usually at races he would pin his number on upside down or backwards. He would pinch his waistline. "Got this spare tire with me in case of a flat," he would say. Today there hadn't been any of this.

Near the starting line, the runners were taking last sips of water from a hose, kneeling down to double knot shoelaces, sprinting last sets of strides. Jenny jogged toward the start, her calves tight and resentful.

Her coach had said that she had raced too many times between September and June. With no strength left to draw on, she had had a disappointing middle-of-the-pack finish to Nationals. Now she was home from school to rest and run long, easy miles. No road races this summer, her coach had said. Take time away, gain five pounds, sit in the sun, relax. She hadn't had time to do any of that. She was still white, drawn, and tired.

But a week ago her father had been excited when he told her about this run. "I have a race for you Saturday," he said. "The new development out in Lake Asbury is sponsoring a mixed-couples relay."

"A what?"

"A two-person 10-K. Men run the first three miles and women the second. Best combined time wins. What do you think?" Her father handed her the race brochure.

"In Lake Asbury?"

Lake Asbury was lumber land, north of town. But the little photos in the color brochure showed green stands of pine trees and palmetto paved through with black asphalt roads. A glossy map promised condominiums, tennis courts, an Olympic-sized swimming pool and a manicured golf course—all surrounded by a five-mile jogging trail.

"Buddy Creighton needs a partner," her father said. "You remember Buddy, don't you?" Buddy was a friend of his from work, a young fellow, 29, 30 and fairly fast. "I volunteered you, what do you think?"

"I think I should do it."

"Good," her father said. "I took a chance and registered you."

Then Buddy called Friday night to cancel. His brother-in-law was coming to town or something. He offered to reimburse the entry fee. "Oh no," Jenny had told him. That would be no problem. Her father could run; after all, it had been his idea. But her father wanted to find her another partner. "It's too late," she said. Her father had sat at the kitchen table reading the brochure and running his hand through his hair.

The pale runners were gathering near the starting line. Jenny slowed to a walk. She had run twelve minutes. She pressed a small button on the side of her watch and the black digits reverted to real time. There were ten minutes before the race began, then another twenty minutes before her dad would be through running his half of the 10-K. His best time for five kilometers was 19:35.

Jenny wiped sweat from around her eyes. It was no kind of day for a race. The heat would slow everyone. The summer bake had set in two weeks ago; not even the mornings had any coolness. The air was thick and heavy, a chore to breathe. Exertion in Florida was strictly for November. She pressed the small button again, and the numbers dissolved back to running time. She would run four minutes more, then jog over to watch the men start.

"Hey, Jenny!" A lanky runner turned and strode toward her.

"Hey, Dave." Dave's red and white high school uniform was the same style she had worn three years ago. He had to chop his stride to match hers.

"When did you get home from school?" he asked.

"Last weekend."

"Well, if I'd known you were going to be here for this race, we could of been partners."

"I'm not much into racing this summer."

Dave's eyebrows lifted.

"I'm serious."

"Who you running with?"

"My dad."

"Well, we could of walked away with it. I had a pretty good season this spring. Finished third in the mile at State. You think Southern will give me a look?" His eyes searched her face.

"Gee," she said, "I really don't know who our men's program is recruiting this year. What did you run?"

"4:25 for the mile, 2:02 for the half."

Jenny nodded and dropped her eyes to the road. 4:25 college milers were joggers in the fast lane. Not that 4:25 was slow time; it was practically the women's world record. But for a man of eighteen—and the time differences always amazed her—Dave's best effort was still 15 seconds off the lead pack.

"How did you finish at Nationals?" he asked.

She shrugged.

"Jenny!" He put his hands lightly around her throat.

"In the sixteens for 5000." She shook his hands loose.

"Sixteen what?"

"16:28."

"That ain't too shabby," Dave said. "So you out here today to run with us turtles?"

"Duelling for last."

"Yeah, well, just don't stir up too much dust if you go by Lynn Rozelli. She's my partner."

"Don't worry. It's too hot to run hard. You two can pull out a calendar to time us."

Dave glanced at his watch. "Hey, I'm up to bat."

"Good luck," Jenny said. But whether Dave heard, she wasn't certain. He loped down the road as quickly as he had come.

Jenny finished her warm-up run near the starting line. Ed Fuller, the race director, stood in the back of a pickup truck with a bull horn under his arm. His voice boomed out over the runners. "Well hell yes, the course has been measured. I wheeled off every step—"

Disturbed by the sound of his voice bouncing off nearby buildings, Ed looked up, trying to find the source. Then he noticed that his elbow pressed the volume button on the bull horn tucked under his arm. Recovering quickly, he managed an embarrassed smile and held the white megaphone to his mouth.

"Well, folks," he said, "that's not the type of welcome I had planned for you today." The crowd laughed. "But since I have your attention, we might as well get started. On behalf of Lake Asbury Construction, I'd like to welcome you to the first Lake Asbury Couples Race..."

Jenny looked for her father. Runners had moved from the tent to Port-O-Let lines to gather around the truck.

"The men," Ed Fuller was saying, "will pass the baton to their female partners, who will then go on to complete the rest of the run." He pointed with his bull horn to a green and white banner stretched between a ladder and a large digital clock. "Both men and women start and finish there. After you run, make sure you turn in your finish tickets to the registration tables..."

Jenny stepped up on the bottom rung of the banner ladder and searched the couple hundred faces squinting up at the race director. At the back of the crowd, she saw her mother. The silver on her mother's black camera sparkled as she pinned the number to the front of her husband's T-shirt. He stood impatiently, shifting from one foot to the other, talking and running his hand through his hair. Her mother, nodding, carefully attached each corner.

Her father wasn't very tall, 5'8", 5'9", but Jenny could remember thinking him a giant. His dark-red hair was now threaded with gray that her mother liked to tease him about. Even with his spare tire, he was a handsome forty-three.

"Folks, you can pick up your batons over there." Mr. Fuller pointed toward the registration tent where a number of hollow metal dowels glimmered in the morning light. The dowels were like the batons that sprinters used for their track drills and relay races. One runner would race toward another who crouched with a hand held out behind her, palm up. At the crucial moment of the exchange, the first runner would find a last sip of air to shout "Reach" and would slap the baton in the hand of her teammate, who would grab it and run.

Jenny weaved through the crowd to the back. Her mother waited there alone.

"Where's Dad?"

"He went to get a baton. There he is." Her mother nodded. Jenny's father jogged toward the start.

"Go easy on them, Dad," Jenny called out. Her father looked over his shoulder, frowned and shook the bright baton.

"What's with him?" Jenny asked. "Doesn't he want to run this?"

"Oh, he wants to run, but I think he feels bad—"

"What did he have for breakfast this time?"

"No, that's not it at all. Your father thinks you should be running with someone else. He wishes he had tried harder to find you another partner."

"That's ridiculous."

"Well, he doesn't think this is going to be any fun for you."

"For heaven's sake, I want to run with him."

Her father edged uncharacteristically close behind the first row of runners on the starting line. Ahead of him, Dave talked to a thin young woman whose ponytail bobbed up and down over the stenciled letters of Asbury High.

"Thirty seconds!" Ed Fuller shouted. As if they were cold, the runners bunched together under the banner. Jenny and her mother backed off the road. The thin runners jumped up and down and ran short sprints out over the chalked starting line. These runners would sprint out under the five-minute mile pace. Other runners would place themselves in the pack accordingly. Her father usually started halfway back, but today he waited, bent slightly forward, behind the front runners. Dave leaned out over the starting line and gave a thumbs-up sign to someone in the crowd.

Ed Fuller held a gun in the air, his arm pressed to his ear. "Runners set," he yelled, then fired. Two hundred rubber-soled shoes rasped across the sandy pavement; one hundred runners left in a confusion of arms and legs. The motion of her father's baton sent the sun into Jenny's eyes. When she looked again, he was lost.

The starting area was strangely empty and silent, full of loneliness of the spectator. Was this what her mother always felt? Jenny shaded her eyes with her hand. She could see her mother's white bloused and blue-skirted figure standing on the side of the road, experimenting with the focus of her camera.

Jenny wiped her sweaty face and jogged toward a water hose. The temperature had to be high eighties. Three minutes had elapsed on the digital clock. The first runners should come back past the mile mark at around five minutes, maybe more. The heat would take its toll. She reached for a water hose.

"Here they come!" someone shouted.

Dave led the first pack of runners back toward the mile mark. Trailing his long, eager strides, a group of runners spread out like a small flock of migrating birds.

"4:49, 4:50, 4:51," the timer read their splits over the bull horn. The pace was quick. Dave looked easy. Spectators shouted encouragement as the runners hurried past. "5:10, 5:11," the timer continued to read from his stopwatch.

Jenny jogged down the road in the opposite direction of the runners racing past. Her dad shouldn't come by for another minute or so. But ahead, her mother waved an arm in the air and bent to focus her camera. Jenny's father raced around the corner. A man running from something. Her father leaned into the turn, pumping his arms, moving faster that he had ever run. His baton flashed in the sunlight like a signal mirror. His dark-blue shirt was soaked through black and plastered to his chest, a fish pulled from water. What was he doing? The pain of his pace was in his half-closed eyes. "Good going, Dad," she called out as he ran past. His eyes were fixed on the road ahead. She should have said more, less, told him to slow.

The timer called splits as her father passed the mile mark. "5:31, 5:32." Her stomach tightened. 5:31 was thirty seconds faster than he had ever run a first mile in a race. He would pay for it. His body wouldn't let him get away with putting it into such an early oxygen debt. His arms would go numb; his legs would become wooden. His heart would. . .Crazy man. She ground her nails into her palms.

"What's he doing?" Jenny shouted to her mother.

"Your dad's running up with Sam Van Wort," her mother said. Her camera had slipped off her shoulder and swung from her hand near the ground.

"I know it!" Jenny felt her scream a whisper. "He's running too fast, too early."

Her mother stared down the road where the runners ran. Adrenaline made Jenny's face tingle. The taste of metal filled her mouth. Crazy man. She shook her head, turned and leaned into a hard stride.

Sprint, then jog. Sprint. Jog. Her pulse quickened, but her legs ached. The digital clock read 10:07. Maybe another ten minutes before her dad would come in. She sprinted again from the starting line. Another stride and she jogged back. Pony-tailed Lynn Rozelli waited under the green and white banner. Only another four minutes for Dave. Her dad might be out there eight minutes or longer. The bright black road was empty for a long time.

"Here comes Dave," someone shouted. "Dave's the first one in." Dave pounded to the start-finish line, almost running up Lynn Rozelli's back. Lynn grabbed the baton as Dave sent her off with a "Go." Then he bent double and sobbed for breath.

"That was 16:02 for Dave Williams," Mr. Fuller announced over his bull horn.

Other men began to come in and hand off to their partners. The large digital clock flipped its bright yellow numbers, 17:16, 17:17. After that first mile her father would be hurting. He might fade badly; he might have to walk in. Jenny bit her bottom lip. 18:01, 18:02. More than twenty women had grabbed their batons and started down the road. 18:26, 18:27. The bright numbers blinked down. She considered doing a few more strides.

"Jenny!" Her father's voice struggled as he ran into the starting area. His head turned from side to side, his chest and shoulders heaved. "Jenny!" He rasped for breath between colorless lips. His eyes teared against the sweat; he could not see her.

"Here," Jenny shouted. She ran to him. He needed to keep moving. Don't stop and you won't overheat. Keep walking; don't let the lactic acid pool. Someone needed to tell him those things. But her father stretched out the baton to her, every muscle straining in his face and arm. She reached for it and ran.

Jenny stared down the road into the wavy heat. Before she realized it, she had passed one, two, three, four, five women. She ran out of control. Too quick. What are you doing? You're running crazy as he did. The thought of her father's race made the dull pain in her lungs feel good. She could see the small crowd as she sprinted around the corner to the mile mark.

"23:44, 23:45." The timer called splits as she passed. They did not make sense. She looked for her father, her mother. There were only other faces. She surged again and passed more runners. Too quickly, she knew. She wouldn't be able to hold this pace. Pace, think, pace. Control. Stride-out. Her calves pulled and threatened to knot. The last time her legs had felt any good was back in April. She had peaked too early for the races that mattered.

She ran wide of the aid station at the two-mile mark and shook her head no to the race workers. No drink. No hose spray. She surged past a group of women running together.

"Get her, Jenny." It was Mrs. Van Wort. "Lynn's the only one."

Jenny ran with pain in her lungs, now in her legs, now everywhere. She might slow. She might quit. She might scream. If only there was enough air.

Ahead was Lynn. Red and white. Ponytail. Jenny surged; her legs balked. The green and white finish banner waved her away. Lynn's footsteps were faster. Go. Faster. Lynn had skinny elbows. The hot sun bounced everywhere. Then there was just her father's face.

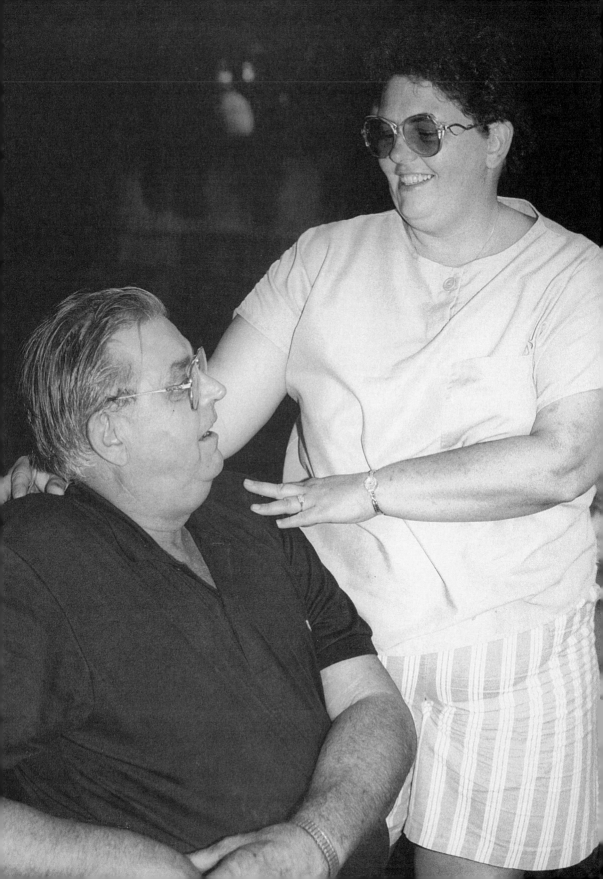

Cartoonist

Nancy Berg

for my father

I am a two-dimensional character
in one of your cartoons.
For twenty-four years, you have been
carefully going over me in ink.
It is taking longer than you thought.

There are mistakes in this drawing.
Some of the lines extend too far
and some are way too dark.
I told you I knew of a magic eraser,
and now you sit,
watching the illustration board,
waiting for heavy black lines to
lift off,
hover in mid-air,
and disintegrate
right before your eyes.

Sandra Gregory

The Prophet's Daughter

Elizabeth Follin-Jones

How tired I became, following
city to city while he preached.
I handled mail, his moiré robes,
reams of tracts, a thousand meals
since Mother died boneweary.
Because He spoke to Father.

Everyone crowded him, I'd
wait for hours in the back,
unnoticed, until they left:
Your father is great, he saves us,
chastises sinners. Such power.
You're lucky, a prophet's daughter.

If He speaks to Father, why not
to me. Last spring near these oaks
I began to listen. Sun swathing
the green, wind in my pores, I heard
dissonance, breath, one voice
like Mother's, then sheaves

of words. You can't imagine
how they fill me, the peace.
Later I stood at a meeting,
said: I too hear a *voice*.
It told me to speak, to tell
the women their worth,

the men their strength,
the children their growing.
They heard. They return.

The voice never lets me down:
Speak of forever, mention
sunwarmth, tell them jonquil.

Now I teach while Father keeps
track of names at the door,
carries in pamphlets. He gives
a short talk but they flock
to my words, lessons
they wish to hear.

Words for a Long-Gone Father

Teresa Noelle Roberts

A certain cat of legend saunters back
Out of the woods to its abandoners.
The family may move to avoid it, but it follows,
Crossing the country on sore, homesick paws.
You never came back
To any of your families.
Like any father cat, you are a myth, a wind
That rumpled my mother's fur and disappeared.

The legendary tomcat cats around.
Like him, you never cared to stay rooted.
You'd been sold away too young, unweaned,
Still an eyes-sealed kitten.
You lost the warm instinct
That guides one home.

I am a restless animal like you, given
To nocturnal prowling. I am no housecat, and impatient
With those who would tame me. I am your daughter.
But I am afraid to end like you, always a stray,
Knowing nothing but the loneliness
Of the cat that walks by itself.

Lori Burkhalter-Lackey

heritage

Anita Skeen

driving south on route 60 at dawn he would say to me,
my chin hooked over the back of the front seat
a few inches from his ear,
thinking how the lines in the back
of his neck were like the deep gullies
that cut through the back hills,
a tense laugh in his voice
"there's where your old man puts in his time"

narrow pipes spit fire at the morning
as ovens cough up white-hot coke
rows of stacks, choking
belch out circles of thick breath
holding my nose, swallowing
even closing my eyes
does not help:
i still drown
in ammonia and smell
that same smell woven into the fiber
of his heavy wool shirts
it fills our house
when he enters each night
and moves with his hands as they
pass food at the supper table

in dreams i climb
thin ladders on those big tanks
my bones against their bones
my flesh freezing, weeping
in the winter cold
to toss my orange hat far up
far out above the webs of dark steel

A Man of Many Hats

Therese Becker

He has a cherub tattooed on the inside of each calf and he used to make them dance for me when I was a kid. He and Mom have gone together now for over thirty years.

I used to wake up regularly in the middle of the night, his deep voice questioning, "Your mother and I want to get married — is it OK with you?" I gave my permission at least once a week for years, and prayed for a good night's sleep.

He never spoke to any of the boys I dated until my husband came along. Bob, miraculously, would extract a singular "hello" from him upon each meeting right up to the day of our wedding. I'll never be able to discuss nuclear war, racial issues, feminism, literature, or my artist friends with him; actually, not much in the world of words has ever passed between us.

I've never called him Dad: neither of us would know how to handle that. My kids call him Uncle Tom, although my son Mike says Tom's the only grandfather he's ever known. A few birthdays ago, he gave me his prized antique telephone, and I was amazed he would part with it. He instructed me, "A gift is not truly a gift unless you give away something you really want for yourself."

When he and Mom started dating he drove up in a variety of convertibles, which through the years he's exchanged for vans and boats. Always a man of many hats, it never occurred to me how bald he really was. Now in his 60s, and with even less hair and a full beard, he's blossomed into a graying Buddha. Why he's even come to cherish a friendship with a cat — something none of us thought could happen in only one lifetime.

I grew up on this ex-Navy cook's food, so leaving the kitchen for my husband and sons to fiddle in seems natural to me. Tom even loved to do dishes, as he said it was the best way to get his plumber's hands "really clean." He still loves to cook, drink wine, collect antiques and paintings of naked ladies, and renovate old houses.

In fact, he and Mom are contemplating making a bid on an eerie 1920 house on Michigan's Lake St. Clair. It is in desperate shape! They know it will take a lot of work and time, maybe more than either of them has left to give, but as Mom says, "I could spend the rest of my life there and be happy, and once we're finished, we'll really have something." When I tell Tom I think the place might be haunted, he just smiles, raises his thick brows and says, "Probably is."

Measuring the Months

Marion Goldstein

He counted and measured his steps
walking me down the aisle
out of his life and into my own.

Sunday afternoon visits he would sit
at the kitchen table,
dicing celery and carrots
for the evening salad he knew I loved.

Now he is counting the months,
twenty-one he says
since last I visited him
measuring them against snow piled
below the window and tomatoes
staked in the back yard turning
from hard green to fleshy fruit

that he carries across the miles
to my house, filled
with his grandchildren
and I wonder as I open the brown paper bag
ripe with his offering
what ritual I will invent

what offering bring

when I come to measure months
by snow piled below my window
and the years blossom
and fall from the vine.

In My Father's Fields

Nancy Frost Rouse

Tobacco rows loom
higher than my head.
Flowering tops
fill the summer heat;
green leaves wither
in the broiling sun,
sickly-sweet as sweat or gum.

Your cursing pits against
the tractor's roar.
Words throb
in the noon sun,
strike like hot, heavy rain.
Thunder rolls through
angry years,
lightning always at our backs.

I walk again
in furrows deep and wet.
Another spring swells
slowly in the ground.
We tread these fallow days
together, hip deep in weeds,
still not knowing
it is ourselves
we're pulling up
root by severed root.

When these fields are mine,
I will plant them
in barley, corn, and wheat,

Sandra Gregory

reaping all we knew to sow,
and leave behind the bread
we could not eat.

My Father's House

Willa Koretz

The building is flat,
   white,
    opaque.
The windows are black,
     impenetrable.

Someone lives in there;
Has been seen,
    from time to time,
Coming and going
From these rooms.

Impenetrable.
   White.
   Black.
A personage with no shades of grey.
Or skeletons in his
    Unfathomable closets.

Retirement

Amber Coverdale Sumrall

My father calls to invite me to his retirement party.
After thirty years he is going out in style,
two hundred people for dinner: newscasters, directors,
big business representatives.
The president of CBS is flying out from New York.

My father is seventy.
The company wants young blood, he tells me.
Retirement means spending time with my mother,
driving her to the market, doctors, church.
He is afraid she will fill his days.

No wives were included originally, he says.
But your mother started a revolution.
This does not sound like my mother.
Is she finally beginning to change?

He tells me the party will be black tie.
He knows I hate parties.
You can wear whatever you want, he says.
He knows I may show up in jeans.

The family will be transported by limousine
to Chasen's in Beverly Hills.
We will be seated on a platform,
everyone will be drunk.
A typical Hollywood Roast:
sarcasm and insults under the guise of humor.

I avoid Los Angeles like the plague.
Feel like a turntable playing 33s at 78 rpms;

can't shut down enough to adapt.
I've had my wallet stolen at Disneyland,
my suitcase lifted after three minutes on the curb
of a quiet residential neighborhood in Santa Monica,
my car side-swiped on the San Diego Freeway.
My marriage barely survived a trip
through the San Fernando Valley.

I know you are probably busy, he says,
hearing the hesitation in my voice.
I have never felt his arms around me,
only anger and disappointment at my refusal to conform.
We have never gotten to know one another,
no time for breakfasts, dinners, weekends together.
He has been working all his life.

Who are all these people, I ask.
CBS invited them. They told me I could choose twelve.
But Dad, its *your* party.
The company is paying, he replies.

I will regress to twelve, say all the wrong things.
Only this time I'll say them deliberately,
be ruthless in my accusations to the chairmen
of Standard Oil and the henchmen of mainstream media.
After every toast I'll yell, Nicaragua Libre.
I will do none of these things.

The company needs to know how many are coming, he says.
I want to tell him I'd much rather come down
for this extravaganza than for his funeral.
As far as I'm concerned *this* is his going out party.

He asks me again, Will you come?
And I answer, Yes Dad, of course.
Of course I'll be there.

Father's Dresser

Lorraine Tolliver

Square, brown, ugly,
varnish thick and shiny.
Plastic lace runs
beneath volcanic, sedimentary,
and granite stones
gathered over the globe
by adventuring prodigy.

The mirror tilts in a carved frame
scratched and spotted with age.
At fiftyish, he'd begun at beveled edges:
six children, twelve grandchildren,
Mother at varied years.
Randomly the collection grew—
a new pose, a new condition,
a tag of memory.
Right corner filled in, bottom rows grew,
top left . . .
Last time I saw the dresser,
nearly all the mirror was covered
with young faces grown older,
plastered there with scotch tape.

Father, have you noticed?
You've nearly blotted out your own image.
By next year,
when I come again,
your face may be a memory,
and the search for your likeness
may need to be made
in the multitude on the mirror.

Cemetery Walk

Barbara L. Thomas

Trees
spring limbed
crowd orchard road.
Dad and I
walk
lulled by trills of bird song.
He casually
reminds me
of his reserved plot
in the veteran's corner.
I taste a pale-red cherry
sharp
unripe.

In Search of Eels

Elisavietta Ritchie

"Hi, Daddy, let's take a walk."

It's a June day in Virginia. My father puts his hands on the arms of his wheelchair, whispers something I can't understand. I try to help him up but he is limp, resistant, heavy.

"Come for a walk, Daddy. Please."

The breeze billows white curtains into the room. The lawns have just been mowed and the fragrance of grass wafts inside.

He shivers, murmurs something about blizzards. Then, slightly more audibly, "It's cold, I'm tired. Can't we go home now?"

Suddenly we're far beyond Lake Shore Drive, in a part of the waterfront I've never seen before. December, Chicago, I'm five, and cold. One mitten's lost. My feet are tired. His legs are longer, he walks too quickly through yellowing snow, gritty slush, toward buildings like airplane hangars with cavernous mouths. Menacing.

He begins to tell me about ships and cargoes.

Usually I love to listen to his stories; he knows about everything in the world. But I've had enough walking. "I want to go home."

"Just as far as that warehouse." He strides on. "Right foot, left foot, you'll see—we could hike around the whole of Lake Michigan. Come on, hold my hand—*Forward, march!*"

"I don't want to hike around Lake Michigan."

But we reach the warehouse, shed he calls it, though it is 100 times bigger than any shed in anyone's back yard. By the pier beyond are big boats: tugs and freighters and tankers and tramps. Huge anchors. I keep hoping someone will drop them with a splash into the water. But the ships are docked with thick hawsers, nooses to choke the pilings. Funnels and cranes. Crates taller than my father sit on the wharves. Sunday and no one is working.

Suddenly the nearest freighter bellows from her funnel and I jump. From excitement, I insist, not fear.

This is the most exciting place I have ever been. I could walk along here forever. At least until I find out how to get aboard one of the boats.

Smaller sheds now, smaller boats, a green diner. Odor of fish, and smoke. We enter a shack. Barrels of brine, string bags of clams, crates of fish laid out on ice, their eyes terribly wide.

"Daddy, look at that snake!"

"No, that's an eel," says Daddy. "Smoked. We'll take a chunk home for supper."

"*I* certainly won't eat that!"

"All right," he says, and carries the smelly package. As we walk back, he tells me about migrations of eels to the Sargasso Sea: how eels come down Dalmatian rivers and swim across the Mediterranean and then the whole Atlantic, and eels come from the rivers of North America, too, until they reach the warm Sargasso Sea. Here they spawn, though I'm not quite sure what spawn means. Then the baby elvers swim back to the native rivers of their parent eels. My father explains that spawn is the proper word for something my grandmothers say people aren't supposed to discuss. But about eels, that's okay.

"Someday I will take one of these big ships. No," I correct myself, "a real ship with sails—and steer it to the Sargasso Sea."

He warns me that in the Sargasso Sea, the rudder, or the propeller screw, might get stuck in seines of floating algae. I'd never get home again.

Home is already far, Lake Michigan is too large, and although he sings old army marching songs to urge me to pick up my steps, toward the end of the journey he lets me ride home on his shoulders.

Back at last in the apartment, he unwraps the eel, opens his Swiss Army penknife (though he could have used the big kitchen knife) and slices carefully.

"I won't eat it," I say firmly.

"Try one bite, just for me."

"I won't like it."

While he hangs up our coats, finally I test one crumb. Awfully smelly, smokey, and salty.

He goes into the kitchen to heat milk for my cocoa, and tea for himself in the samovar from Tula. I test one more sliver. Then another.

He returns with the steaming cups. The eel is gone.

Because it is Sunday and I am five, he forgives me.

*   *   *

Later, I am seven, or twelve, or fifteen. We are walking along the canal, or a river, or best of all, a beach. I mostly keep up. No eels now, but we see frogs and ducks, water snakes, minnows. He tells me about everything in the world. We talk about fishing.

Sometimes at the ocean we cast from a rock or pier or the beach, though it is always the wrong bait or wrong tide. Or we drop handlines over the side of somebody's boat. On rare occasions, we catch a keeper. Then he takes out his Swiss Army knife and teaches me to gut, clean, and filet. His hair sparkles with scattered fish scales. So does mine. Often we spread a picnic: black bread, smelly cheese, a tin of sardines. I eat only my share.

At nineteen, during my college vacation, I fly out to join my parents in Japan. My father and I climb Mount Fuji. High above the Pacific, and hours up the cindery slope, we picnic on dried eel, seaweed crackers, cold rice wrapped in the skin of an eel. He reaches the peak first.

Through years we hike along a beach in Cyprus, beside a river in Lebanon, the Seine, Alpine streams, and picnic by various other waters and weathers. We overtake one another. I've never known anyone with such energy.

*   *   *

Time rots like old fish.

Today in the nursing home in Virginia I beg him, "*Please*, Daddy, just a little walk. You are supposed to exercise."

The nurses are supposed to walk him daily, but they are always too busy. I try to walk him whenever I visit, but seldom lately has he felt up to more than a step or two.

"Come, Daddy, forward, march . . ."

He can't get out of his chair: I've forgotten to untie the straps of the "posey" which restrains him. Not that he often gets up on his own, but once in a while he'll suddenly have a spurt of strength, then is like to topple over. I crouch to lift his feet from the foot pedals, fold back the metal pieces which too often bruise his paperthin skin.

"Come, now you can stand."

He struggles, but cannot move. I place his hands on the rubberized handholds on the metal walker. "Hold tightly and you can pull yourself up."

He grips the walker and struggles forward. He still cannot make it to his feet. I am about to lift him, when the nurse comes down the corridor.

"Lunch trays are up," she calls out. "Everyone hurry to the solarium!"

As if anyone here could do much hurrying.

I push his wheelchair to the dining room. His plastic plate is heaped with pureed tuna–he's been having trouble swallowing lately—but he ignores his lunch. The ice cream turns to milk in its styrofoam dish.

I hand him a spoon. It slips from his fingers. Some days I sing him old songs, tell stories, but one of the residents turns the television on full blast and he can't even hear my repeated, "Won't you eat, Daddy, please?"

I lift a spoonful of grey fishy stuff to his mouth.

He whispers, politely, "I don't care for any."

Nor would I.

Suddenly I go into action, wheel him to the nurses' station, sign him out for the afternoon. It has been a while since I've taken him out, the weather has been too cold or too hot, I haven't had time between work and children and travels, he has had so many bad days of late, he has often been asleep when I've come by, it's a hassle to get him into the car, and how much would he take in any more anyway.

We head fullspeed for the elevator, downstairs, out the main door, out into the parking lot. An orderly helps me get him into my car, and fits the folded wheelchair into the trunk. I adjust our seat belts.

Off we go, down the road, over the bridge toward town.

"We're crossing the Potomac River now, Daddy. Ahead are the Kennedy Center and Watergate, and to the right—can you see the Washington Monument? Remember when we climbed up there, ignored the elevator? And the Smithsonian Museum—how many rainy Saturdays did we spend in museums? And look at those flower beds—"

He doesn't say much to my running travelogue, but seems to be staring out the car window and taking in at least something of a scene he used to know well. The sky is very blue, and so is the river.

We turn south from Independence Avenue past some warehouses and pull in by my favorite wholesale fish market.

"I'll be back in a moment, Daddy. Please wait for me—"

As if he had a choice.

Inside the cool building men in hip boots are sloshing around carrying 16-pound sea trout by the tails. Fish scales fly through the moist air. Frozen boxes of squid and string bags of clams are awaiting pick-up for some restaurant. A curly-haired man is hosing down the floor. I step over the puddles and ask him if by any chance he has any eel today.

"We haven't had any in a year, Ma'am. But it just happens that today—if you don't mind smoked eel—"

He wraps a large chunk in waxy white paper. I pay and hurry out to the car where my father is watching with interest a forklift loading crates of mussels into a truck.

"I've brought you a surprise."

"Why, thank you, dear!" His voice is stronger than I've heard it for months, and he stretches forward for the package with interest. He loves presents, and reaches with awkward fingers to try to open it. The smell fills the car. His fingers can't undo it, but he holds it while I drive down to the river and find a parking place near the marina. Somehow I wrestle the wheelchair from the car, set it up, wrestle him into it, push him out to a level area.

"I'd like a bit of a walk," he says clearly.

Gradually I lift and push and pull him to his feet. Now he is standing, unsteadily, then gains a sort of balance.

"See, you made it! That's wonderful...First take a deep breath...All right? I'll be right behind you, my hand is in the small of your back. Now—Forward, march!"

He shuffles a couple of steps along the quai. I am holding him securely, somehow maneuvering the wheelchair behind him in case he gets tired. I steady him as he pauses to watch the sail and motor boats on the river. He manages a few more steps, and a few more, along the quai. He hasn't walked this far in months, and seems pleased with himself. There is a small bench ahead and, abandoning the wheelchair, we sit down together.

Again for the first time in months, he begins to talk. He remarks on the red dress of a buxom young woman striding by, he wonders what day it is, he inquires about the children. It is some sort of a miracle, this return to "normalcy," however brief. I cherish every instant.

"And what about your dinner plans?" he asks with his old graciousness, and invites me out for supper. Of course I accept, we'll manage it somehow. Meanwhile, it is only mid-afternoon, too soon for restaurants, but he has worked up an appetite.

I run over and buy something like lemonade from a vendor. Then I take the small smelly package wrapped in glazed ivory paper from its plastic bag.

"Look, Daddy. The fishmonger actually had some smoked eel."

We unwrap it, then I take out the Swiss Army knife my stepmother gave me "for safekeeping," open the bottles and thinly slice the silvery flesh.

"What a beautiful picnic," my father beams.

He takes a swig of the lemonade, then with steady fingers picks up a slice of eel and downs it without difficulty. Then another, and another, until he eats the whole chunk.

*   *   *

My father was given an extraordinary service at Arlington Cemetery: honor guard of 100 men, rifle volleys, six white horses pulling the caisson, and one black horse riderless with stirrups reversed. Two weeks later came the memorial service in the Russian Church; so beautiful, especially with two bassos in the a cappela choir. Following each service, a wake at my house, for which I laid out his favorite caviar and herring with sour cream, curried lentils, salads, sausages, cheeses, and sweets. But I could not find an eel.

Abacus

Karren LaLonde Alenier

In the last months he
became a monk—
shaved skull
eyes wide
or half-closed
robed in
deep lines
cheeks and brow
arcing a silent O
abiding night
counting days
a column
of stone
his will
reckoned
to tell
his daughter
nothing

Clothing

Rose Rosberg

My father was a garment presser: all day he stood,
a Russian Jew, huge-handed; bearing down hard,
he steamed the creased apparel in a New York factory.

Now his work has been taken over by death,
which has smoothed my father's wrinkled face
and blurred its marks of rough wear
from loss of jobs, strikes: his skin
is loose enough to slip off his flesh.

As he lies flat on his bed, absorbed by dying,
that mouth which yelled about union violations
is closed now, quiet as velvet.

His hands rest at his side, they are held down
by that taker of finished products from workers,
their final boss, most expert disposer of garments.

Empty

Ursula Hegi

Seashells I gave to my father,
a green braided bookmark,
drawings brought home from school,
the soft feather of a yellow bird.

Later I sent him photos of my wedding,
shirts and sweaters, books,
letters with the pictures of his grandchild.
Thirty years of gifts.

But all he kept
locked in the safe next to his will,
is the empty shell of a teddy bear I don't remember.
He says I cut it open as a child.

Portrait

Lynn Buck

I best remember him
in summer blue seersucker
and crisp cotton shirt with striped silk tie
properly knotted
under stiffly starched collar,
white handkerchief properly edging his pocket.
Strict Bible-reading teetotaler,
Perfection was his goal,
from neatly spaded garden edges
to exact margins for typewritten pages,
straight lines for his transactions—
and, for his daughter, straight A's
a requirement.
Miscast as mundane salesman of insurance,
he was an enthusiastic pusher of life—
eloquent talker, words spilling out, overflowing
endlessly,
known at times to talk to himself
when nobody else would listen.
He should have been a professor
or a politician, perhaps a preacher.
Soft of heart, with great expectations
for the human spirit,
he would give away his last dollar
with exasperating ease
or co-sign a bad mortgage for a friend
at the drop of his cocky straw hat.

Too soon, in his sixty-sixth year
that fragile life strand snapped,
frayed and worn thin

by the intensity of his reality,
the reality that taught him:
"We are put here for a **Purpose**,
our duty to fulfill
through toil and perseverance
and Power of Will."
His words I have cross-stitched
on the sampler I call my soul.

Seldom did I see my father idle,
rarely did I hear him laugh.

Inheritance

Cinda Thompson

by the eldest

Rows of corn so orderly
But life is not
Orderly, death is.
In the end all returns to
Calm and silent land, so much
Ground to be planted green.
It is the steadiness of life,
It stuns me,
The steadfastness with which
I now must try,
I long to think, how long
Did my father think of death
As release. No more
Rows to be dug,
Homes to be built, maintained.
This earth is but
Darkness to be turned
And I will, but I will still
Not find my father.

Mothers
&
Sons

I Knew It Was a Boy

Nancy Bengis Friedman

I knew it was a boy
from the beginning.
The night told me so.
I grew bigger and bigger
as if a prize-winning fruit
bloomed red and green
inside of me.
"It's a boy!"
the Italian ladies on the block
would croon.
I'd smile.

The day our baby was due,
a boy was born across the street.
Eight days later,
a bris.
I went, eager as an eighth grader,
watching for the first time
a frog being dissected.
I took the rabbi's card.

Two weeks later,
our bris.
New York grandparents brought lox,
whitefish, sturgeon, bagels.
Boston grandparents brought chairs and danish.
Invited brothers, cousins, menfriends
were sick, away on business
or having nervous breakdowns.
I was there
watching my son strapped

Phillip Shelton

to a plastic platter,
sucking a hanky
dipped in purple wine.

I leaned forward.
The corpulent rabbi told the story
of the first covenant, Abraham's first promise,
read the ancient blessings.
The baby sucked as the rabbi pulled the swaddling cloth
and did his job with a shiny steel blade,
his "messah."

I'd labored 24 hours
howling like a poisoned dog,
silently counting 1-10, 10-1
in Yiddish to numb the pain.

I don't remember penis #1
vs penis #2.
I remember his scream and my nonchalance.
I knew it was a boy.

On a Night of Rain

Beryle Williams

Leaning down
to kiss the boy goodnight
   small arms reluctant
   to break the circle
   that enclosed her head,
   their special blend
   of body scents, and rain
she thought of paring down,
whittling off the nonessential hours
that smother spare, core minutes.

Resting a moment
against him, remembering
   her body once arced
   around his newborn form
she drifted toward sleep
dreamed of carving
herself into
a small wooden boat
a simple ark, perhaps
   the kind a child might carry
   in a secret pocket
   seaworthy
   forever.

Phaeton's Fifth Birthday

Penelope Deakin

If I were a mother
in Sparta
I would learn the sleeping
weight of my son's head
on my arm
the rhythm of his questions,
only to lose him
to the sweat
and shouts of a man
who sleeps too heavily
to hear a boy's voice
cry out from a dream,
who sees immortality
in the play of muscles
down a young man's back.
I could only stand and
watch the yellow leaves
gather in the quiet backwaters
of a river.

John Renner

Troubled Sleep

Linda Quinlan

He is small for his age,
a look-like-me boy
with knowledge of crawling animals,
unusual animals living under his bed.
The floating fears come to him;
they are drawn to both of us.
In the darkness we curl under the blankets
in our separate rooms.
He is saying over and over to himself
that at eleven
he is too old
to run to his mother,
but asks if he can lie with me—
he is not very tired.
In a few minutes
I carry him asleep
to his room.

He owns you with the fears,
the child that wants you home
to entertain,
licks his fingers
after you bought the wrong
kind of cookies again,
and leaves you for a party
when you've decided to stay home.

When my parents went out
Uncle Ed would call me up.
He would ring the bell
and I had to let him in,

a relative, I couldn't be rude.
He asked me to sit on his lap,
told me I was sweet,
so special that he came
just to see me
growing up to twelve.

When my son cries at night
I wonder if he could be either
my uncle or me.

Sometimes a Son

Janice Townley Moore

Sometimes a son
will surprise you   come to sit
on the side of your bed
where you lie with a broken leg
everyone else seems to have forgotten
He will balance three pieces
of grape smeared toast
on a too small plate   drink orange juice
from your best crystal   You don't mind
this particular morning   the first sun
flashing off the leaves outside your window
He will tell you his funniest stories
fragments of toast   crumbling
onto the sheets   You will not brush them away
Your son will tell you these things
you've heard before
They will seem new now   as beside you he
shakes your whole bed with his laughter

Optical Illusion

Maxine Combs

Most of the time I am a perfect wife and mother. But it's the other times I'm going to tell you about, the times when I switch roles. As wife and mother I do all the conventional things: I fix dinner, I carry down dirty dishes from upstairs, I shop, I support my husband's career, I'm even gracious when his sister comes from Pittsburgh for the weekend. I also attend PTA meetings and watch my daughter play soccer on Saturdays. My daughter is always going somewhere, and I am always picking her up. To a friend's house. To the dentist. To her music lessons. She plays well, although she rarely practices; these days she is working on a Mozart sonata.

"You need to practice at least forty-five minutes a day." Legions of mothers before me have said it.

"I'll do it later," she replies, also sticking to the conventional formula.

She's a lovely girl, everyone says so, and I'm in the forefront of her admirers. The effortless quality with which she performs charms us all.

"You're doing a wonderful job."

"She's delightful."

"She plays beautifully."

"She's a honey."

I sit back and observe her smooth progression through life as I rake in the compliments.

My husband is also a person to be proud of. He makes documentary films that everyone admires. Films on political candidates. Films on national parks. Films on artists. He works hard, travels extensively, earns a high income. Besides his professional success, my husband is kind, thoughtful, emotional, but not arrogant. He helps with everything around the house: cleaning, cooking, the laundry, you name it.

At least once a month one of my friends says to me: "You have everything. The perfect life. The best of all possible worlds."

Lori Burkhalter-Lackey

I smile and nod yes, and my eyes agree yes—I am one of the charmed ones—yes, the wheel of fortune does keep turning up my number.

But I promised I'd tell you about the other part of my life, the non-perfect part. I live in this part with my son, and together we try to maintain a low profile.

My son does not do well. He was kicked out of the Boy Scouts. It looks like he will fail the sixth grade. His new bike got stolen the first week he had it. Once he got picked up for shoplifting a pouch of tobacco at Dart Drug.

"What kind of tobacco?" I asked.

"Skol."

We discuss the Scandinavian origin of this name.

"Let's play tennis," I say to him when he comes home from school, before he can tell me the current day's disaster.

We go to the courts.

I love to play tennis. I love to be outdoors, I love the sun, I love the feeling when the racquet wallops the ball. I am only a mediocre player, but my ego is easily satisfied. Most of the time I can still beat my son.

My husband does not play tennis. He is too busy. Last month he was in Utah for two and a half weeks filming. He reports the film is coming along.

My daughter also has a full schedule and no time for tennis. Besides, she prefers to do things with her friends.

So it's just me and my son out there on the court flailing away. After we've been hitting a while, he'll say something unreal like: "I think I'm getting pretty good. I'll bet I could beat Billie Jean King."

"Just play," I advise. "Billie Jean King would not hit you one ball you could return."

"I could too return them."

"How was school today?" I don't really want to know.

"All right." He hits a two-handed backhand. A few minutes later he adds, "I have detention on Thursday."

"What for?" I dread the answer.

"Singing in Social Studies. We had a substitute."

"Poor lady," I say, thinking back to all the substitutes I had in school and the trouble we used to cause them. One of them, I remember, once ordered a rowdy kid to sit in the wastebasket. "If you're gonna act like trash," she screamed, "I'll treat you like trash!"

That is one of the few incidents I remember from school. The rest of it was days to be pulled off the calendar, one after another. I daydreamed through my classes. I still daydream.

After tennis we buy Pepsis. It has to be Pepsis so we can check the bottlecaps for a prize. Last week we got one that said: Instant winner, .25.

My son believes he will win the grand prize. Or win a bike to replace the stolen one. He was also an avid player in the Safeway Bingo game and in the McDonald's Build a Burger game. We won a dollar from Safeway which we forgot to collect, and two cokes and an order of fries from McDonald's.

My husband once sat Larry down and explained the odds against his winning a major prize. Something like 1 in 100,000. Larry listened carefully but still believes he can win. He believes that someplace a buried pot of gold awaits him.

My husband claims Larry is too naive for this world. I like it that he uses the word naive instead of immature.

Larry got kicked out of Boy Scouts because he and a friend snuck off from the group on a camping trip and pitched their tent several miles away by a river. The rest of the troop spent hours searching for them and worrying.

"We wanted a real adventure," Larry explained.

"This boy is irresponsible," the Scout Master said. "Besides, after a year in the Scouts, he has yet to earn even one merit badge."

Irresponsibility is a word I am familiar with. My mother used it about me, teachers labeled me with it at school, and much later a psychiatrist selected this word to describe me in his notes. He claimed I didn't take myself seriously and probably he was right. I went to this psychiatrist, Dr. Kessler his name was, for about five months. For me it was not a useful experience. I went because people kept implying that I ought to be more successful, that I ought to "take control of my life." However, I remained content to drift. Or, if not content, resigned. The prospect of taking control confused me, and I saw no reason to try unless I absolutely had to. I didn't have to. It was clear to me that I was a person without special talents, that it was all right to sit in a corner and leave center stage to those with stronger wills, firmer plans.

The only hitch is Larry, who, as far as I can tell, is doomed by his heredity. He has absorbed my *laissez faire* philosophy, whereas from his father he has inherited the desire to excel. He wants to be top dog, but competition gives him headaches. He wants to play tennis with Billie Jean King, but he refuses to take tennis lessons. He would have liked to become an Eagle Scout but he couldn't earn even one merit badge.

I try to think of a solution to this problem. In the meantime Larry floats on a thin piece of ice in a rough ocean. My comfortable, accommodating drifting is not for him.

Momentarily I expect he will sink and dissolve and whatever is left will wash away from me. Then I will be left alone with my high-achieving daughter and husband, the perfect wife and mother, performing my lonely duties as cheerleader.

I try to resist these thoughts. As an optimistic fatalist I believe that eventually all things will work out. So if Larry is scattered and sunken now, I see him someday restored and made whole like one of those ancient buried corn gods who reappear to give life in a later season. With this thought I shelter him as best I can, mourning both the necessity and futility of my illusion.

In the Clerestory of Leaves

Barbara Crooker

We drive to your special education preschool
under an arch of maples, half green,
half turned to gold,
the dark branches bold as the ribs
of a great cathedral, flying buttresses
that bend the light.
You haven't changed in the last two years,
developmentally delayed, mildly retarded,
school a struggle to stay in your seat,
say the beginnings of words,
point to colors and shapes.
While you wrestle with scissors,
daub with paste, I sit in the hallway,
trying to write, turn straw into gold.

When our two hours are spent,
we drive back up the hill toward home,
see the stand of mixed hardwoods
in full conflagration: red-gold, burnt orange,
blazing against the cobalt sky.
The architect who made these trees
was sleeping when he made this boy.
And my heart, like the leaves, burns and burns.

Rite

Elizabeth Eddy

my teenage son was
just a normal youth
we hadn't brought
pot up the river
from New Orleans with
us when he was 12
months old and no
one seemed to know of
LSD but maybe Huxley
far away who wrote
of mescaline

so to expand his
mind and take
himself into another
dimension he played
his 78s on 33 the
Rite of Spring
four times a day
and it did and
he was and
I was
too

Mrs. Portnoy's Song

Joanne Seltzer

Why do I love my son?
Why not?
What other man will ever penetrate
the seat of my emotions

as deeply as my son did?
I have marked every part of him
top to bottom
inside

and out
with my own indelible handprint.
When I call him a lout

he acts like a lout.
And when I call him a prince
he acts like a prince.

Character

Rachael Beck

What a drag it is
to build that kid's character!
I know it's better for him
if he learns
to clean the sink and tub,
wash dishes,
take out papers and cans for recycling,
and return those returnable beer bottles.
I know it's important for him
to Learn Responsibility at home;
but I'm exhausted
by the time I ask him,
persuade him,
coerce him,
listen to him tell me
he'll get to it—whatever the request—
as soon as he gets a break in his homework,
his music, or during the next TV commercial,
and then he doesn't move
till we go through it all again!
How long must I build his character?
When may I just do the chores
myself?

Nothing to Eat

Rina Ferrarelli

I went out and left him to scrounge
for supper, thinking
he'd had enough at the Steelers game,
and I wonder now
if he'll remember this
when he grows up,
instead of the meals I prepare
with salads and fresh fruit
because he doesn't like cooked vegetables
if he'll remember coming home
to a dark, cold house
with "nothing to eat"
and forget that he used to brag
to the friends he brought home for lunch
about my "famous" fruit cups.

Second Son

Margit Moore

You are the one who looks like me
You were always here
Preconceived

The child that backs up
Digs in
Holds tight

Even my anger at you cannot be simple
Shaded by sadness for that other child
Who felt extraneous

But you are the one who looks like me
The smell, the feel,
the shape that is familiar

Nothing is simple between us

Phillip Shelton

Scorpio Child

Bonnie Michael Pratt

Light and dark; anima and animus—
we dance and wait and dance again.
I long for this drama to end.

Your frenzied needs are echoed in me,
child with dark November eyes,
left on the doorstep of my life
while I waited for surcease
that never came.

But through all the harshness
there is a feeling of wonder,
so out of place I cannot look at it.
Something I need to know is here—
an alchemy we will work together

When you have betrayed me the last time
and the moon is rising in Scorpio again.

Lori Burkhalter-Lackey

Somebody Else's Child

Bettie Sellers

When you borrow money
(and I know I'll
never see that thirty
bucks again),
you're somebody else's child!

And when I find your
sweaty jogging pants
behind the sofa cushion
in the den,
you're somebody else's child.

Or my pillow breathes
the faint aroma of Obsession
(and I've been out of town
for a week, and don't use
perfume anyhow!)
you're definitely
somebody else's child!

But when you cry on my shoulder
after midnight
and we end up talking
about your dreams,
I know, no matter what,
you're somebody else's child
and mine!

Sticks and Stones

Barbara Lau

Editor's note: This is the first section of a novel that examines a seven-year-old son's reaction to his mother's abrupt death.

The way the story went, Father wanted to give him a scuffed-shoes, small-town Texas name like Hank or Will. But Mother was determined to name him Mario after her eldest brother.

"*Hank.* Can you imagine that?" she would scoff years later, rubbing white caliche dust off the nose her son had inherited from Uncle Mario even without his namesake. "Where is there beauty in a word like Hank? Sounds like someone who drinks out of a trough!"

They finally settled on Anthony, though Mother always pronounced it "Antony" without the h and Father ended up calling him "Son" most of the time. His sister simply called him "Brother." She was named Lily because she was born on Easter morning. She arrived three weeks earlier than expected, while Father was on the road somewhere between Dallas and Waco. So that time Mother got to choose the name without any interference.

Lily was Anthony's only sister. At least she got a name that fit her, he often thought. She resembled Father with her thin stem of a body that freckled lightly on her shoulders and knees each summer. Her hair was the palest blonde, capable of turning nearly white under the fierce glare of the Texas sun. The skin on her face was petal thin, with the veins in her cheeks clearly showing beneath the surface. And when she became excited, or angry, or overheated—which occurred with great regularity many times each day—her cheeks would turn a startling shade of scarlet, bright as strawberries lying in a white porcelain bowl.

Though he never openly complained about his name, Anthony secretly concluded that he and his name were a poor match. When he was old enough to wear his first tie and accompany Mother to mass, he learned that there was a dead Italian saint named Anthony. But he doubted he would ever become as perfect. Then there was a Mark Anthony who had lived a long time ago, but he soon forgot what exactly the man was famous for after Mother was no longer around to tell him. "I think you are growing up as handsome as Mark Antony," she used to say when her son dressed in his red tie and blue and black checked blazer for church.

For some reason never explained to him, Father rarely went to services with him and Mother. And Lily was too young to sit through the sermon without whining, so it was just the two of them on those precious, candle-scented Sunday mornings. Anthony didn't mind Father's absence as much as Mother seemed to. In fact, he preferred to have Mother all to himself after having to share her with Father the entire weekend.

He was also glad for the house to get back to normal on Monday after Father drove off to his job selling tractors and combines around the state. The house always changed when Father returned home late Friday afternoon. Sometimes it grew stiff and quiet, like at church when a prayer was being said and everyone was hunched over on their knees. Father's presence, and the sight of his huge white shirts and underwear flapping abruptly on the clothesline, changed Anthony as well. Somehow his mouth talked less than usual. His hands grew soft and clumsy, especially when Father threw a baseball to him or handed him a hammer. At times like that Anthony wondered if Will or Hank would have been better names for him after all. And if, having those names, Father might have loved him more and misunderstood him less.

Anthony wondered, too, if Father minded that he took after Mother. They both had dark, thickly curled hair, gnarled as a bird's nest. Their skin was the color of lightly toasted bread. At the age of seven, Anthony's feet and hands still looked too small for his frame while his nose looked much too big, but Mother promised that all his parts would catch up with each other eventually, though she could not say exactly when this miracle would occur.

Actually, when Anthony stared at himself in the bathroom mirror, he concluded that he looked like neither of his parents. He questioned why he could not simply look like himself. But grown-ups were always saying things like, "You're the spittin' image of your Mother," or "You sure favor your Momma."

He thought he resembled his Mother in more important ways than looks. Like her, he loved going barefoot, squishing cool pudding-like mud between his toes, digging in the pungent, lime-green garden, feeling the intense Texas sun massage a tingling yellow warmth into his bare skin. He also loved learning the names of all the flowers in Mother's garden: zinnias, petunias, verbena, vincas, painted daisies, and Oriental poppies. But to Father and Lily, they were simply "those yellow flowers," or "those big pink things."

Anthony thought he possessed his Mother as surely as he possessed the cards in his baseball collection and the coins in his piggy bank. No matter how busy Mother's hands were with her bread dough or scissors or yarn or garden hose or the hundreds of other things that occupied them, they would quickly find their way back to him whenever he needed them. But this was seldom the case with Father. Anthony often had to wait for him to respond to his questions and requests, as if Father had to think twice before answering him. On occasion, he would even look at Anthony with a half-second glaze of confusion, as if he could not quite remember what connection this child—the one waving at him by the curb, holding up a long-stemmed zinnia, waking him from his nap—had to him.

Anthony also noticed the strange look of longing Father had on his face when he watched Lily nonchalantly burrow under Mother's skirt or saw Anthony plop on his mother's always receptive lap. Father's face looked the same on Sunday afternoons at the neighborhood swimming pool when Mother shared her ice cream cone with Lily. Mother never seemed to notice or care who got the next bite. Because to her, feeding Lily was the same as feeding herself, and letting Anthony throw pennies in the fountain was the same as doing it herself. But Father seemed to need permission to lick Mother's ice cream cone or to lay his head in her lap when they watched TV on the couch.

Anthony thought that Mother's feelings were so inseparable from his that whenever she did deny him complete access to her, it came as a shock to him. He would feel the invisible twine that connected them suddenly jerk, then slacken. And for an hour or two he would feel unbalanced, like a table with a shortened leg. It happened sometimes on Saturday mornings, when the door to Mother's and Father's bedroom was closed and locked. It happened every time he would enter a room and their conversation would abruptly stop. He felt the same chilling stomach-jerk on the nights Mother would prepare an early supper for him and Lily, then hurry them to bed as she made a different-smelling meal for Father and her. Anthony knew she was not meaning to punish him. Yet he could not think of any other reason for excluding him from her presence.

On the other hand, when Father's attention and face and lap were unavailable to him, it did not surprise him at all. As long as he could remember, his father's responses had been contingent upon certain key phrases and intonations. Phrases such as "That-a-boy," and "Good catch!" meant Anthony had won his attention for a few moments. And though Father rarely spoke harshly to him, his words did not have the comforting lilt and sway that Mother's had. Instead, Father's voice had an opaqueness, an imperviousness, to it. Unlike Mother's liquid golden tone, Father's was black and white and punchy, like the sound of chalk on a blackboard.

Still, Anthony believed that his father loved him. But his kind of affection was very different from Mother's tightly wound love that never slackened for long. Once, when Anthony questioned her about it, she clutched him to her so fast that she didn't stop to wipe her hands on her apron. "Of course he loves you," she said. "It's just that a grown man's way of loving is harder to see, like a secret. Just trust me he does. And, after all, you're his only son."

Anthony did not doubt her. Yet when Mother went shopping by herself on Saturday afternoons, leaving only Father to look after him and Lily, Anthony always felt a little anxious.

The San Antonio Times Herald could not print Mother's long beaded string of names in the article. The paper's policy was to use a maximum of three names per person. This was particularly prudent in a town that, in 1958, was nearly fifty percent Hispanic, many of whom had names even longer than Mother's.

After the funeral, Anthony insisted upon keeping the newspaper articles in his treasure box in his room. Every few days he would implore his father to again explain the reason for printing a shortened version of Mother's name. Mainly he wanted to hear Father recite Mother's six-part name, fearful that he might forget one of them. The idea of losing his grip on any part of her was frightening to him.

"Maria Rosalinda Lorca Garcia Mauter Brown," Father would say, enunciating every syllable in a husky, louder-than-necessary voice that barely suppressed the pain and impatience he felt. "There, son, are you satisfied now? Why don't you go play with your sister for a while and let me pay attention to my work. I've told you before, I've got to finish all these forms."

Anthony knew that these morning recitations annoyed his father. But hearing her long, exotic string of names spoken out loud had become a kind of magical formula for him, an incantation for bringing her back home.

Rocking in Mother's chair in the middle of the night, staring at the vacant face of the moon, he repeated her name over and over with the rhythm of the chair. He would rock and rock and chant her name until he finally felt moored to the only spot in the house that felt stable and safe.

During those first few months without her, he often wondered if she might have been more circumspect had she been christened something calm and sensible, like Edith Mayfield or Doris Cook, his second and third grade teachers. Both had white hair and pillow-plump arms. Both had managed to live a long time. Surely they would have remembered to look both ways before crossing the street, Anthony thought. Surely they would not have risked riding a bike in a thunderstorm.

But Mother's name had a restless, untamed sound, as if not meant for someone who believed in ironing bed sheets and saying bedtime prayers and unfolding a starched white linen napkin on her lap at dinner. Even when Brown was added, like a plain red caboose, the Maria-Rosalinda-Lorca-Garcia-Mauter part thrashed around Anthony's head like a pigeon caught inside a chimney.

At first he had blamed Grandma Mauter for Mother's daring behavior. Then he remembered how Mother had told him that a name was really just a word, harmless if you did not take it too seriously. "And words can't hurt you, like the sticks and stones rhyme says," she used to remind him, reciting the rhyme whenever he complained about the kids calling him "Tony Baloney" and "Phony Tony" when he stepped up to bat.

Still, his concern with Mother's name would not fade. After the funeral, Father and Grandmother Brown were forever repeating and spelling her name on the phone. And for months, letters, seed catalogs, magazines, and packages arrived with her name printed on them. Occasionally her name bolted out of the car radio or TV, when the announcer talked about the worse flooding in San Antonio history.

Yet he had never worried about his mother's maiden name until she died. In fact, he rarely heard it. Until then, Father called her "Honey" or "Mother" most of the time. He was also fond of inventing an ever-evolving list of nicknames for her. At Christmas she became "Rudolph" and "Plum Pudding" and "Miss Santa." In the spring he named her for whatever new flowers she was trying to coax out of the acidic caliche soil—bluebonnet, snapdragon, gardenia, any floral name except for lily, which of course was already taken. And in summer, her perpetually bare feet and mass of black hair tied back in a multicolored scarf prompted him to call her "Gypsy" and "Magpie."

Of all the nicknames father conjured up, Anthony's favorite was "Abominable Snowman." It originated from her habit of showering a layer of flour on the kitchen floor each afternoon. She could not be bothered with using measuring spoons and cups to prepare her homemade tortillas and biscuits. Instead she would plunge her hands into the flour bin (one, two, three, four handfuls roughly equaling one cup) and fling the flour into her bowl. This sparked an explosion of fine powder that settled on her eyebrows and hair and blouse and the floor. Inevitably something would distract her attention before she could remember to sweep it up. Then she would walk out of the kitchen carrying the flour on the soles of her bare feet.

"Oh no! The abominable snowman is loose again," Father would announce when he arrived home Friday afternoons and found her tracks up and down the dark wood floors. That meant Father had made some profitable sales and was in the mood to play their game of tracking Mother. "Must be a preeeetty biii-iggggg creature to have such faaaatttt feet," he would shout in a gruff voice. "Wonder where it could be hiding?" Then Anthony, Lily, and Father would stomp around the house, opening closet, cabinet, and bedroom doors, making roaring sounds in unison, and banging on kitchen pots to scare her out of her hiding place. Finally they would find her, crouched behind a piece of furniture or curtain.

It was just a simple hide-and-seek type of game that Father invented the last year Mother was with them. Anthony knew that other boys his age had outgrown such games. But he could not resist playing this one, because he relished the feigned look of surprise on Mother's face when they finally cornered her, because he loved being gathered up in the warm, prodigious circle of her arms. At the time he had no way of knowing how indelible her tracks would be.

Planting Rose Bushes

Patricia Garfinkel

With rain threatening, my son and I struggle
with the hairy roots of three rose bushes,
hoping to get them in the ground before the storm.

It is April and I have wrenched our roots
from the firm ground of family to dangle
in space and time, unable to catch hold

of new ground, unwilling to return to the old.
My son trembles holding onto the roots
and to me in the cold. I tremble holding onto

my reasons, hoping they will grow new roots.

Lori Burkhalter-Lackey

Someone Could Do That

Donna Trussell

I remember the funeral better than I do Mother. 1927. I was just a little boy at the time. It wasn't foggy, like I thought it might be because of this funeral in a movie I saw. No, it was a beautiful day. It didn't seem right. Two beefy guys shoveled dirt on Mother's coffin, and all the while the sun shone and birds flapped around and sang.

Neighbors came to our house with chicken and apple cider and cakes. Cars were everywhere, even on our yard. The sofa was jammed with people. Dining room chairs were lined up in a row, and that's where my brother Weldon and I were. We just sat there, doing nothing. Once Weldon started kicking my foot, but Dad told us to settle down. My baby sister was the only one who got to run around.

A pecan pie sat on the table. No one was paying any attention to it. I thought it could be hours before they broke into it. This old lady with a hairnet on came over and patted my knee. Her hands were cold and bony. I could see the veins.

People filled up the guest room and my room too. Weldon and I were supposed to sleep with Dad in his bed. He told us to be quiet so he could get some sleep, but he didn't go to sleep. He got up and walked into the living room.

Then Aunt Vesper walked by in her quilted pink robe with burns on the sleeves, the one she wore at breakfast whenever Weldon and I stayed with her. She'd cook us pancakes and stack them on bright yellow and blue plates that said "Hand Painted" and "Italy" on the bottom. I loved Aunt Vesper. When I'd ask her to do something she'd say, why, I'd be glad to. She'd smile, instead of looking put out.

I heard Aunt Vesper and Dad talking in the living room. Dad cried and said it was all his fault. How could it be Dad's fault? It happened at Aunt Pearl's, miles and miles away. Mother went swimming in a river and drowned.

I figured that with Mother dead and Dad crying, I could get out of bed without worrying about a whipping. I walked in the living room and asked Dad why it was his fault. He plunked me down on his lap and told me about the night I was born.

I didn't think about Mother all that much while I was growing up. But sometimes I did. All these mothers in their perfume and lipstick would show up for Open House at school. There was a curlyheaded one with rouge on her cheeks and eyes that took it all in. She'd go "Oooooo" and "Aaaaah." There was one who squeezed her little boy's hand so hard her knuckles turned white.

I didn't feel sorry for myself. I didn't know I was supposed to until I got old enough to talk to girls. They'd ask me about my mother and father, and I'd say Mother was dead. Then their faces would fold up.

I never talked about her. There wasn't much I could say about Mother anyway, since all I remembered was that she painted. She had a closet with a window, and that was her studio. I smelled turpentine whenever I walked by.

One day we were supposed to go to Aunt Vesper's, but we didn't make it and Mother was mad. She put my sister in her crib and sat me down in front of it. "Don't move an inch, and don't make a sound," she said. She went into her closet.

Weldon and I sat there for the longest time. We heard the other kids outside playing cowboys. Finally Weldon whispered that I should ask Mother if we could go now. I knocked.

The door flew open. "I told you not to make a sound," she said.

She whipped us. Weldon and I sat on the rug and watched patches of sunlight inch across the room until Dad came home at six.

By the time I got to high school I wanted to see Mother's paintings, stored at Aunt Pearl's in the Panhandle. I was to inherit one. "Your mother left us a note," Dad said. A will? "No, just a note." But why did she write a note? How did she know she was going to drown? Dad just turned away.

I heard about a teacher who assigned square roots and then didn't show up the next day to collect them. He'd hanged himself.

People said how he didn't drink and didn't run after little boys, how he was the last person in the world they thought would do a thing like this. But other people said they saw it coming, that he'd been talking about moving to Mexico.

I decided to ask Aunt Vesper what she knew. One day I was patching her roof, and she came out and squinted her eyes and said I'd done a good job. I fiddled with my tools and worried about how she'd take what I was about to say. Finally she started walking back to the house. I caught her arm. I asked why Mother killed herself.

Aunt Vesper looked at me a long time. For a minute I thought she was going to try to talk me out of it, but she just shook her head. "No one knows. We asked that question for days."

How could Mother do that, just end it? I always thought dying would be like a pen running out of ink. It writes and writes for all it's worth, and then it sputters. That's when I'd think about how great and terrible it's been. All the big and little things I'd done. The time I jumped a boxcar and lived like a hobo all the way to Albuquerque. Or later that week, when I walked to Aunt Vesper's to give her the Indian ring I'd bought her. The rocks under my feet were as hot as metal, but the breeze felt good. I'd think of things like that, as long as I could. I'd stretch it out.

I tried to pump more information out of Aunt Vesper, but she wouldn't be pumped. "What your mother did was selfish. Sinful. Leave it alone."

I wrote to Aunt Pearl, and she wrote back that I could come get Mother's paintings anytime I wanted. I wasn't twenty-one yet, but she didn't care. "I think your mother just wanted you kids to be old enough not to tear them up."

The bus ride to Aunt Pearl's was as dull as school. I looked at farms and cows, but that was only good for half an hour. I imagined the sky full of paratroopers. I'd heard that snipers shoot paratroopers, and they die before they hit the ground. Still, I thought sailing through the sky and seeing the whole world spread out before me sounded better than anything that could happen to me hanging around Texas.

My girl wanted me to wait till I got drafted. "I won't think you're a coward," she said. I hated that word. Sometimes I wondered if that was Mother's problem. That's what our preacher said about people who did themselves in.

It was still light when the bus pulled into Plainview. It was plain, all right. You could have set up a hundred outdoor bowling alleys with just some paint and pins.

At the bus station there were a couple of women waiting. I tried to figure out which one was Aunt Pearl. I picked the lady wearing dark stockings and a blue hat with white feathers. I was wrong. Aunt Pearl turned out to be a fat lady in a wrinkled dress with flowers on it. Every color of the rainbow, and then some.

How'd you know me, I asked after she came charging up. "Well, Brice, how many big, handsome fellas do you see getting off that bus? Just you!" She hugged me like a wrestler.

Aunt Pearl looked at me sideways while she drove. It made me nervous. I decided I'd better think of something to talk about. I was going to tell her about a grass fire I saw on the way to Plainview when she started telling me about her truck. Then she told me about her farm. We crossed a river and she said, "That's where your mother drowned." Just like that, like she was still talking about chicken coops. I figured she'd tell me everything.

"What happened that day? Before Mother did it, I mean."

"Not much. Except that she asked me if I'd look after you kids. She wanted a job."

"What did you say?"

"Why, I said no, of course. I had four kids of my own. Nobody blamed me afterwards."

"Why did she kill herself, do you think?"

"Well, everyone in the family had a theory, and there were twelve of us in all. But one thing we agreed on was that your mother was spoiled. When us kids had to work in the fields, Ella would say she had a sore throat or something piddling like that, and she'd get to stay home with Ma. Ma loved us all, but she had a soft spot for Ella."

I tried to fit this new information into the fuzzy picture of Mother in my head. I had a bad feeling. I tried to enjoy the sunset, but I couldn't. I didn't like it that Mother had tried to get rid of us.

When I got to the house I met Uncle Calvin. He shook my hand and crept off somewhere. "I guess you're anxious to see Ella's paintings, so let's have at it," Aunt Pearl said.

The attic was crammed full. Shoe boxes of popsicle sticks. Old wrapping paper and bows, "too pretty to throw away." Lamps they bought and then thought better of, or just got tired of. A sewing machine we had to step over.

In the corner I saw Mother's wedding veil, just like the picture on Aunt Vesper's mantel. A hundred white beads and tiny green leaves.

"I'm going to let you mess around," Aunt Pearl said. "This dust is getting to me." She clomped away.

A painting leaned against the wall. Roses. But there was something odd. Aunt Pearl had told me that Mother didn't have canvas, so she'd paint on whatever she could find. And these roses were painted on brown paper, like a grocery sack.

I flipped through the pictures, and each was like the last. Wreaths of roses, every one. I'd imagined them so many times that the real ones looked small and plain to me. I guess I'd been hoping that these paintings would prove Mother was a genius or something. That would explain everything. But Mother's roses were dark. Almost black, some of them. Damned ugly, if you ask me.

I rummaged around in her trunk and found a picture. Mother's head was tilted, and her fingers were touching her chin and neck. She was smiling, just barely, and her eyes looked right into the camera.

I found some clothes and books, not much else. I was almost ready to go when I opened her Bible and something fell out. "By the time you find this, I'll be gone."

The note. I sat down and planted my feet in front of me. Then I evened my heels up. I listened for Aunt Pearl, but all I heard were the soft insect sounds of night falling. I must have folded and unfolded the note ten times.

"I'm tired," the note said. "To my children: I gave you life and that's all I gave you. Anything else you get is icing."

It hit me like a slap. How could she say it's okay that my baby sister never knew her mother? That Dad's heart was broken? And me. She turned her back on me, just like she shut that closet door.

I slipped the note back in the Bible and put it back where I'd found it. I arranged the paintings back like they were. I turned around, tripped on that sewing machine on the floor, and shut the door forever behind me.

I said goodnight. Aunt Pearl protested. "Don't you want to stay up and talk? You had so many questions in your letter. Aren't you even gonna eat some supper?"

I shook my head. You can't punish a dead woman, but I was going to try. For the next twenty years I never asked about her. For twenty years I thought of other things.

I went to war. Then college. Then I married Janine. I didn't make much money at first. Janine and I, we just had two pans. We didn't even have one of those things you put dishes in after you wash them. Janine would lay a towel on the counter and put the dishes on that. I told her to go ahead and splurge, but she'd just smile.

Now we have lots of pans and dishes. The kids are all grown up. People started dying on me. Aunt Vesper. Aunt Pearl. Pearl left me a thousand dollars "in case Ella's death was my fault in any way."

Ella. I hadn't thought about her in so long. Christ, I thought, did I really make such a big deal about that?

When my daughter asked questions about Ella, I didn't hesitate to tell her the truth. It occurred to me—yeah, someone could do that, do what Mother did. Get married, have a kid, and then walk away. Just walk away.

My daughter, she tried to put this women's lib interpretation on the whole thing. Still, it unnerved her. That same day she asked me if I had my life to live over again, would I still have kids. Sure, I said. "Even after all the trouble we caused you?" I said that someday I'd probably even the score. "But wouldn't your life have been simpler if you could have concentrated on your career instead?"

Boy, I really hooted at that. I told her my kids will remember me after I'm gone. The people at work, they won't remember me. Hell, some people walking around that place now, young fellas, have no idea who I am or what I've done for that company. They think I'm some old coot still hanging on. But my children, they'll remember me.

Summer Custody

Pamela Ditchoff

This September, the onset of your
thirteenth year,
you returned with more of him;
taller than me,
hair on your upper lip,
bulge in your racing stripe sweatpants,
and defiant strut.

The eyes are still mine,
nose, mouth, cheekbones;
but your voice harbors a deep secret,
whispered to Cain and Abel, to Abraham,
every man to son.

This summer he told you.
Angry with me for shaping you well.

The secret must be something huge,
saved for the vulnerability of puberty,
the season which aches the ribs of men.
A bone of contention to separate
mother from son.

A Sweet Sad Turning of the Tide

Maude Meehan

My two young sons
move with assurance
through the maze
of ropes and sails,
steer out of turbulence
to calmer seas,
drop anchor.

They climb the mast;
my body tenses
with past apprehension.
Suddenly one dives,
I plummet with him,
breathe again
when he emerges.

The small boat pitches
as he hoists aboard.
I glance up swiftly
to the swaying crossbeam
where his brother
perches, confident.

As heavy mist rolls in
they guide the light craft
back to harbor, and like my hands
old maps lie folded in my lap.

Reaching the laddered dock
they stretch strong arms
to steady me. When did
this turnabout occur?
I have become a passenger
on their journey.

My Son at the Wheel

Mary Balazs

Evening's cold tarpaulin over my shoulders and lap,
my teenaged son at the wheel,
I sit stiffly in the low convertible,
grimace before deep potholes, blind curves.

My son tightens his grip. I gaze among forest trees.
Here and there are tall poplars, a maple's shapely crown.
Elsewhere are chestnuts oddly bent, alders strangely formed,
as if obstacles to growth had forced trunks,

lengthening limbs astray. Expansion created
wasteful loops, costly curves, precipitous breaks,
occasionally lethal twists. My son grins:
I have not chided him for speeding up,

am ignoring dust clouds heavy in our rear.
Gravel spins beneath accelerating tires.
I stare past receding trees, the car's polished hood,
where the turtle, strayed onto the road, was saved,

the groundhog at the highway's edge unhit,
the arc of leaping deer complete.
My son shifts into high gear.
A rabbit, in the nick of time, hops away;

a cardinal swoops before the radiator grill.
My right foot presses an absent brake.
My son holds the accelerator to the floor, his sights
on other routes: crowds, the mainstream's haste.

Sandra Gregory

Heather Smith

Katharyn Machan Aal

Sometimes I think I'll die. The door
begins to rattle, handle
almost seeming to turn. I think

it's him, come home. My son, gone
almost a year, his name
a sweet I keep upon my tongue

as I live now for his letters.
So few! *My Dearest Mother,*
To think of all of you with winter

heavy on the eaves, and me
here on this island, hot
sun every day, salt water blue

and sparkling so it hurts the eyes
to see. Oh, I imagine
every street of that warm place,

the trees with coconuts, the big
brown birds that carry fish
in pouches, the fort, the other boys

and men in uniform, the ships
that do not bring him home.
He says he cannot write of what

he's doing there; the army forbids
such news even in peace.
So I get palms and pelicans,

nothing of what he's become, no word
of his return. A year!
I'd like to send you oranges,

he says, *and limes that come here from
the mainland, but I'm afraid
they'd spoil, fresh as they are.* Instead

he's sent a silver sugar bowl
for me, and for his sister
a china-headed doll and tiny

forks and knives and spoons, *salvaged,*
he says, *from a wreck and bought
at auction very cheap.* So now

I'll drink my coffee every day,
his gift before me, pretty
thing that mocks me whispering

*Anderson is far away
and is not here and is
not here and will not be again.*

Feathers

Alice Bloom Fuchs

for Josh

I try to become accustomed to your stubbly chin, the teenage eruptions, both on your skin and otherwise, your disappointment that the color of your '73 Chevy is orange like your hair, that all the money you earn as bus boy goes for gas, that it runs best when you drive like an old farmer.

I wash the tomato stains out of your workshirt, smiling. In the "pumpkin express" you chauffeur around your friends with experimental haircuts, experimental stomachs and lungs, experimental feelings. One of the kids you don't chauffeur around has a 4x4 and thinks he's cool. He experimentally runs down our favorite hen. You want to throw her body in the back of his truck but I say wait. Dig a hole. When he roars by he'll see three feathers stuck in a mound of dirt. The wind will cry through them like angels. But he will never hear. You hate it when I talk like this.

I boil an egg for you. I don't tell you it was hers. Don't beat him up, I say, don't continue. No, we can't afford a 4x4. We can't even afford the pumpkin. When the car finally starts you are late for school. I watch your pesky exhaust tumble down the road. So many feathers.

Ode to My Son's Forgotten Cap

Lu V. Smith

Take this cap;
It is a nice cap,
The color of a sand pile
On a wet day.
Usually it perches placidly
Atop a young man's head,
A fungus taking nourishment
From the red hair and gray matter
It clings to.
A young man and his mushroom
In a personal relationship
A warm togetherness.

But that was yesterday . . .

The cap lies limp,
Unattached,
Denied life
By the entrance of Eve,
Lulling into forgetfulness
The male ego;
Hypnotizing the senses
With her swinging hair
And large red hat.

And this is today . . .

Hang this cap
In its closet cell;
Treat it gently;
It is a nice cap.

Son's Wedding Day

Marilyn J. Boe

He polishes the '72 Buick bought from Mom for the buck it takes to transfer the title, and he rubs coat after coat of wax on its rusted lemon finish in overlapping circles.

It shines, sleek as a butterfly, both doors open like wings waiting to fly him away in four hours, and what can a mother say to him when he spends his wedding day in the driveway, suds cascading over bald tires, blue SOS foam on his shoes. He takes hours to do what she knows can be done in 37 minutes.

This isn't the first time he's left her. That happened years ago on a summer day suspended in heat, a day when Mom won too many checker games at the picnic table in Bemidji State Park, and he walked away kicking pine cones until long shadows nudged him back to her quiet tent.

During his long-legged years, he sold his Ludwig Drum set, cymbals, bongos, cases with casters, rolled his years of music out of the house in exchange for a used Kawasaki he hid under a sheet behind the shed, its ghostly outline reminding her of the worst that can happen to a boy on a motorcycle. He roared away from her warnings.

Today his vacuum cleaner whines, turning the Skylark into a cave no speech can reach. Soon he'll yank that last blue vein of extension cord from the garage wall, step into his silence, float his golden wings down Morris Lane, leaving behind a scrub bucket and three gray rags, the last residue of his cocoon.

Lament of the Bridegroom's Mother

Ellie Mamber

Lulled, I thought him safe.
But he was in a twinkling abducted . . .
abducted, I say, though he
offered his hands for the binding,
smiled as he was led off,
glad to live among strangers,
to live among them
with their unimagined ways
and forget his own
and his true self.

My son has been stolen by
gypsies, to live in their
rough dwellings and roast
wild meat on an open fire,
know simple thoughts and
coarse laughter, forget
his own ways.

My son has betrayed,
has gone to their camp
by the railroad tracks,
and I am wild with my rage:
I tear at my hair.

How can I forgive his
strange choosing—
and what, now, of me?

Weekend Visit

Sue Saniel Elkind

I think of nothing
think of everything.
I remember when I was a child
how I'd hold my hand skyward
and blot out the sun.

He wants to be somewhere else
but he's here in the house he left.
He has brought a woman with him.
She has no point of reference.
He has told her nothing about me.

My son is uncomfortable.
We are all uncomfortable, not knowing where
to begin.
I'd like to lie down, safely float again
in my mother's warm belly.

I have many questions
but as eyes get used to darkness
my lips make a seam sewn tight.

I want to ask him, "stay longer."
He's already closed the door.
I hold my hand up.
I can't blot out the visit.

Did My Sons Forget

Aisha Eshe

Two Mother's Day cards
are missing from my shelf
I noticed the empty space
when I did my Monday dusting
There was just too much room
for my Pledge-filled dust cloth

Kim's Lot

Randeane Tetu

They were banging and moving machinery down the road in Kim's lot. They had a truck running down there all the time or coming and going. The flatbed truck stayed down there all day while the bulldozer ran over the lot, and pulled out at the end of the day with the bulldozer on it.

The bulldozer started after the chain saws had felled a space for it, one month after Virey had sold it to Jeffrey Smullen at the bank for his son to build a house. She had sold it all of a sudden after waiting seven years for her own son to return, to take up the land of his fathers. She had sold it on a day when to her it seemed more hopeless than usual to wish for him to come home. She had walked in Jeffrey Smullen's office on purpose to tell him he could buy the land, saying, "Yes," instead of, "No, that's Kim's lot," when Jeffrey said, "How about that piece of land?" "Yes," she said. "I think so. You can buy it if you buy it today," knowing she would change her mind, knowing that the changing of her mind would be one other hurtful part to remember about Kim.

She had saved Kim's baby teeth in a jewelry box, had saved them from under his pillow as a reminder that he had been little once and had needed her, saved them as a talisman against his forgetting her.

She had heard enough of Alaska in the first days he was home from the service, and she wouldn't listen to herself when she remembered it was the last frontier. Her father and her grandfather and his and his had lived here, if not in this house, in one of the other family houses.

Virey's brother Vince came for coffee with her every Saturday. When Kim was still in the service, Vince said, "He won't stay." Virey told him what she was going to do, what she'd done, and Vince said, "He won't stay." She had kept the airplanes set up in his room and known he would want more than just a room when he came home. She had subdivided the piece at the end of the property.

Sandra Gregory

And then Kim was back from the service, not back in the way it would have mattered during the war, but back in the way that people suddenly noticed he'd been gone. What he'd done in the service, Virey saw, was to cut the ties he had to home. He didn't put the airplanes away from his room, and she saw he was only pausing in his race to be somewhere else.

Vince drank the coffee Virey made on Saturday and said, "Virey, he has to be. You have to let him."

"But it's so far," she said to Vince. "Why so far?"

Then she and Kim were in the kitchen, across from each other at the table.

"What's wrong with it?" Kim said. He was leaning forward toward her. "What's wrong with it?" He had just come in with the tax bills from the mailbox, and he waved them as he spoke. She wouldn't tell him. He should see that she wanted to have him near her with her grandfather's grandfather.

He left the airplanes in his room and the clothes he'd left the first time, and he went out of town, and he went to Alaska.

Virey waited seven years. She thought that seven years was somehow significant in common law. She decided in a moment that she would sell the land to Jeffrey Smullen whose son Jeff was moving back with his family, giving up his city job to come work at the bank with his father. Jeffrey had a picture of them behind his shoulder at his desk when she went in to sell him Kim's lot.

Kim had sent her pictures of his house, his wife, and two little boys. They weren't real to her. She wondered if he had found some boys who looked like him and posed with them. His wife looked as if she couldn't speak. Virey had never heard her say anything.

Virey couldn't see the land from the house. She felt the noise from machinery kick up against the clapboards of her old house. She didn't know what they were building down there. It wouldn't match the style of her house.

A truck went by with planks, and all day after the bulldozing there was hammering. She didn't know how to build a house. Then later in the week the trucks of fill went past.

Virey waited until evening. She waited until the trucks had gone back past her house. No machines were making noise, and she could hear no hammering. Then she walked on the road down past the woods beside her house to the lot she had sold.

The earth that the bulldozer had torn up was powdery brown, and the trees were down. They had the foundation in and had started on the frame. The sticks of framework stabbed at her, but she didn't move. The woods closed in as the dark came down. The powdery earth stood out light-colored.

The stabbing of the sticks was a sharper pain than the ache she had had waiting for Kim to use the land. Virey stood on the road and the dark crept out from the trees. It was easier in the dark to see what the house would be. Fireflies made their light trails across the darkness in front of the house, and Virey turned to walk home.

She thought she'd have a picture taken of herself posing with the new family, not saying anything, posing in front of the lovely front doors it would have with a man and his wife and their children in the sunshine and send it to Alaska.

Conversation with a Son

Shirley G. Cochrane

He brings me seasoned wood
on winter's coldest day
and builds a teepee fire.

*If I were a Choctaw
and you Squaw Mother,
we couldn't talk like this—
you know, the manhood thing.*

Then how . . . I want to know.

*I'd talk to the fire
and you would overhear.*

The fire he built burns on
long after he has gone.
I bend to catch his words
pulsing within those flames.

Phillip Shelton

A Tar Baby

Ric Masten

she waits in the brier patch
  sweet as honey
  tacky as tar
in her thorny ambushes she waits
and practices her guitar and her
  i don't know
  what you're talking about
song and dance
  till i come along
  her half-witted son
she'd say
  and i would agree
for anyone with a lick of sense
knows enough to leave a tar baby be

still
through much perseverance
    i've learned

ways
to handle the whole messy business
of a child-parent relationship
  and can do it these days
  with a certain dispatch
    and expertise

the safest approach of course
  is to stay out of reach
and when least expected sneak up
  on the snare and yell
    tar baby
    i love you

then run like hell
sometimes i can be two blocks away
before she knew i was there

or if you're a glutton for punishment
you can survive keeping in mind
the fact that you deal
with something as primal as
    the La Brea Tar Pit
  a quagmire of glutinous stuff
    that sucked in
    and gummed up
the fearsome tyrannosaurus
but these being civilized times
   if it seems important enough
  go ahead pay the tar baby a call
    do it
put yourself through it
maybe twice a year
    but that's all
however
never stand outside that door
thinking you know what it's all about
thinking
   this time i'm gonna straighten
    the tar baby out
oh yes
let me say this in closing
my oldest daughter
has turned twenty-two
and someone is coming
    Br'er Rabbit
    is that you?

My Mother's Hands

Geoffrey Brown

I think of you in my travels about the city but especially at the end of a long hard day like this one. I think of your hands (which you once told me you thought were ugly but which I know are so beautiful). They have your life written in them; they have been shaped by the earth you have loved. Your hands! They have dug in the soil, & given it so much nourishment, exactly as much as they have been given in return. They have lived, & been beloved.

Your hands! I love your hands! Those blue bulgy veins you think are "unattractive" are really the blue streams of the high country. They are your ways of worshipping as you work in the Earth, it is your version of the shaping the Great Spirit does, as you are shaped in return. And so are the very life forces shaped as they work through you, learning in *their* turn, &, as it has taken time for this round, this partnership to be formed, so have your hands evolved. It has taken time for them to be distilled, like wine, & to grow, like the roots of trees. Look at the bark of a stone pine or the twisting branches of a madrone. Look at your hands again, & see through my eyes: by God! They have seen all weathers! A baby's hand might be freshly minted & have its own beauty, but it has no soul, for it takes time for a canyon, or a pair of hands, to grow a soul.

I see you shining through the skin of your hands like the sun inside the leaves of your apple trees.

Lori Burkhalter-Lackey

Mushrooms

David Baker

for my mother

Once again, the sun cool in the half-light of trees,
we step down into bottom land and feel the sink
of the earth. Here, between this sheer slope, a scarp
of limbs and rock, and the other one surely rising
through the distant trees (yet out of sight as we descend

the final steps), a river once rolled itself to sleep
and died. We know this from the rock, the shape
of land that's left, *a memory the earth keeps of itself:*
that's what you told me years ago, one spring, when
we first walked these grasses on our search.

It was mushrooms, then, we hunted—whites and browns
that rose like sponges under rot-black leaves,
or luckier, giant reds the size of skulls. For miles
we walked, heads down, and followed every fallen
log along its northern side. Stumps were good, too,

and maple trunks, and best, the grassless ground
beneath the frequent patches of mayapple. We filled
our sacks that afternoon, then stopped looking and walked
until night. The wind carried in trees above us
the faint brooding of a stream we would never find.

Today we've simply come to talk. No bag. No hunt.
Yet to talk we've come back here, spring again,
the land the same, us the same. We are another way
the earth remembers itself. Wild flowers bloom
where they bloomed before, water seeps slowly

beneath our feet—we walk where we have walked.
You point out now a familiar log, white with fungus,
where then we found mushrooms, how they were growing
hidden near that hollowed cave of wood, and how,
even now as you step on one, a dozen more come into focus.

Mom

Reginald Lockett

the cartilage
barely   attached
to the bones
in both knees. her
right arm is weak
        and
gives out   at
the elbow. way overweight,
she's been classified
handicapped, and can't
        get out much
like she
used to. cooking, washing,
cleaning
or anything pertaining
    to work
are misplaced words
in her vocabulary.   food
comes her way
    from relatives
and that new county
program
  for the disabled.
then there's concepción
    who comes in
to clean, console
    and chastise
once every week. though
she shouldn't have it,
        five piece orders
of golden bird

Sandra Gregory

fried chicken,
barbecued beef,
    smothered
in sweet sauce,
    from gadbury's
  and
bacardi light with coke
somehow appears
    through
the good graces of a niece,
nephew, cousin
    or a friend. right there
in the back house
on e. gage avenue in the city of angels
she keeps close tabs
    on
her favorite daytime and evening
        soaps
among old and new photos
        of
three sons grown and gone,
and a grandson and granddaughter
born
  too late in her life
        to
toddle behind her
    in the yard
or tag along to a neighborhood store
anticipating
    the multicolored popsicle
or chocolate and nut covered ice cream bar
rewarded for toting
    a sparsely
filled bag of fruit, vegetables or meat.
fiercely defiant
    in her stubborn convictions,

she sometimes   speaks
        of
that head-on, inevitable
        meeting
with death and how she'd
        like things
        arranged. when
we three sons moan, "ah mom!"
            in
still perfect harmony, she
        chuckles,
cocks her head
        to that favored
right angled slant
        and
looks far off
        into a distance
we three have not yet begun
to travel.

Gathering Mayflowers

Rodrick Bradley

Against the darkness
of the woods, her figure
hunched with pain, my mother
bends to brush aside the tapestry
of winter leaves.

Spring again:
you were always one
for the truth, the sudden tumor
surprised the doctors, us,
everyone but you.

As you bend I see you
face the truth of your not being
here, the truth of passage as you
pluck a tiny cup of spectral light
and pass it to your grandson.

Another spring: your last
and we walk, three generations,
you pointing out for us
the secret brief beauties
lighting up the darkness.

The Ice Man Still Comes

Peter Coyne

In this breaking April weather,
when the winter pond is coming back to water,
the ice man still comes
at midnight to my mother's house.

I hear his wagon horse shift legs.
I hear him chipping out a large white slab
for the upper shelf
of my mother's empty chest.
She orders a hundred pounds a week
and cube by cube he fills her up by flashlight.

Nothing human sticks on this colossal coldness.
The slush veins of my impervious
wire monkey mother
with her frozen glass eye vision,
cold as the walk-in
of a butcher shop on the moon.
Her thin blue face comes through
the small window pane in the door.
She will not let me in.
She shakes her icicle fingers,
the white air flailing at her mouth.

Spring never came to her.

Clues

Father Benedict Auer, O.S.B.

"They say you can tell everything about
a woman by looking inside her dresser drawers."
Yasunari Kawabata, *Snow Country*

Neatly folded undergarments—
slips, only white, in one drawer;
stockings, beige, in another;
things used less often kept
in drawers touching the floor.
It is all so pragmatic:
no frills, no waste.
In the center drawer
a jewelry case is set—
a few semiprecious stones
attached to cheaper settings,
a couple of handmade rings,
and one gold necklace,
expensive, but tasteful,
which could be worn anywhere.
And on the bottom layer of the box
are rosaries—broken segments,
crystal beads, worn out
from overuse, a medal of a pope
long since dead, and
a rosary, unbroken, once
used by her mother,
a box of passed-on prayers.

Red Dirt

Gilbert Honigfeld

Mother, I visited your gravesite
yesterday, and worked in the dirt
that rests on your chest, crushing
those old bones as though death
alone were not final enough.

I worked in that red dirt,
picking out rocks and pebbles,
smoothing out high spots
with the same flat-hand sweep
you used to straighten blankets.

I sowed Oregon perennial rye,
(guaranteed germination 80%),
patting the seed into place with
a hundred left-right handprints,
then sprinkled water from a jerrycan.

When I got home last night,
my shirt was bloodied with
the red dye of your dirt stains,
and the sink-water went carmine-red,
my hands baptized like two old sinners.

This morning, your blood still runs
from my fingers, in faint pink dilution.

About the Contributors

KATHARYN MACHAN AAL was born in Woodbury, Connecticut, in 1952. Since 1975 she has lived in Ithaca, New York, where she teaches on the faculty of the Writing Program of Ithaca College. Her poems have appeared in many magazines and anthologies, and she is the author of thirteen published collections of poems, the most recent of which are *When She Was the Good-Time Girl* (1986 winner of The Signpost Press annual competition) and *From Redwing* (Foothill Publishing, 1988).

KARREN LALONDE ALENIER is the author of two poetry collections, *Wandering on the Outside* and *The Dancer's Muse*. She edited the anthology *Whose Woods These Are* which chronicles eight years of the Word Works poetry programs at the Joaquin Miller Cabin in Washington, DC's Rock Creek Park. She is a winner of the Billee Murray Denny Poetry Award. She's currently serving as President of the Poetry Committee of the Greater Washington, DC Area, which is centered at the Folger Shakespeare Library.

DARIEN ANDREU is a graduate of the writing program at Florida State University. She trains writers and runners at Flagler College in St. Augustine, Florida.

DORI APPEL, a poet, playwright, and fiction writer, is also an actress and co-Artistic Director of Mixed Company Theatre in Ashland, Oregon. Her most recent play, *Girl Talk*, co-authored with Carolyn Myers, was produced in 1988 and is scheduled to tour in 1988-89. Her poems and stories have appeared in many publications, including *The Beloit Poetry Journal*, *Yankee*, and *the new renaissance*.

REVEREND BENEDICT AUER, O.S.B. is director of Campus Ministry at St. Martin's College in Lacey, Washington.

DAVID BAKER is author of two books of poetry, *Haunts* (Cleveland State, 1985) and *Laws of the Land*, (Ahsahta/Boise State, 1981), as well as three chapbooks. His work has been widely printed in literary magazines and anthologies, and he has been awarded grants from the NEA and Bread Loaf. Currently, he teaches at Denison University in Granville, Ohio.

MARY BALAZS is an Associate Professor of English at the Virginia Military Institute. She also works extensively in NEA's Poets-in-the-Schools Program. Her poems have appeared in such magazines as *Mississippi Valley Review*, *Kansas Quarterly*, *St. Andrews Review*, and *Pivot*. Two books of her poetry have been published: *The Voice of Thy Brother's Blood* (Dawn Valley Press) and *The Stones Refuse Their Peace* (Seven Woods Press).

CHRIS BARTLETT lives and works in New York City as a fashion photographer. He tries to take as much time as he can pursuing his "art."

RACHAEL BECK is an Indianapolis wife, mother, and grandmother. Impatient with obscure poetry, she has written for fourteen years what she calls "plainverse." Her work has been published in *Indiana Writes*, *Writer's Info*, *The Poet's Job: To Go Too Far* (an anthology published for the National Association of Poetry Therapy) and *Light Year 88/89*.

THERESE BECKER's poetry, photography, and essays have appeared in many literary journals and anthologies including *The New York Quarterly, Passages North, Contemporary Michigan Poetry: The Third Coast* and *Anthology of Magazine Verse & Yearbook of American Poetry.* She lives in Lake Orion, Michigan, with her husband and three children and teaches creative writing through the Michigan Council For The Arts, Creative Writers in the Schools Program.

NANCY BERG is a writer of poems, screenplays, articles, and advertising copy. Her poems have appeared in numerous literary journals and national magazines. Her professional goal is to write musical comedy, develop her fiction writing, write more articles for national magazines, and expand her freelance advertising work around the country.

MARILYN J. BOE is a poet who lives in Bloomington, Minnesota, with her husband Bill. She is a retired special education teacher of dyslexic children. Her poems have appeared or are forthcoming in *Iowa Woman, Outerbridge, Loonfeather, Great River Review* and others.

JAMES BOGAN teaches film and art history at the University of Missouri-Rolla. During a recent Fulbright Fellowship in Brazil he shot a film about an unusual art form of the Amazon documented in his *T-Shirt Cantata.* Currently he is at work on another documentary film, *Tom Benton's Missouri.* His previous books include *Trees in the Same Forest* and *Sparks of Fire,* an experimental anthology on William Blake.

WILLIAM BORDEN's poems and short stories have appeared in many literary magazines and anthologies. His novel, *Superstoe,* was published by Harper & Row. His plays, which have won several national competitions, have been produced in New York, Los Angeles, and elsewhere. Universal Pictures has optioned the film rights to his play *The Last Prostitute.* He teaches creative writing at the University of North Dakota and is Fiction Editor of *The North Dakota Quarterly.*

RODRICK BRADLEY is a photographer living in Los Angeles. He has published a novel *TV Man* (Holt Rinehart & Winston 1981) and writes detective fiction under the name R.B. Phillips.

GEOFFREY BROWN was a poet from California who was particular loved for his dramatic readings of his poetry. He taught poetry at the Lighthouse for the Blind in San Francisco. He worked as an organizer of community gardens. His collection of poems, *Road of the Heart Cave,* was published by Thrown to the Winds Press in 1984. He died in 1987.

LYNN BUCK is a recently retired college professor turned poet who lives and writes in an old Long Island house called Serendipity overlooking the Peconic Bay. Her work has been published in a number of journals, including *Long Pond Review* and Lake Effect, and in anthologies *Poets for Africa* and *Voices at Serendipity.* She won the open competition of the Westhampton Poetry Festival and honorable mention in the World Order of Narrative Poets Competition (1986).

LORI BURKHALTER-LACKEY was born and educated in Los Angeles, completing her photographic training at Otis/Parsons Art Institute. Her work has been exhibited in many

California galleries and she recently completed several documentary photographic assignments in Paris.

SHIRLEY G. COCHRANE's second book of poems, *Family & Other Strangers*, was published by Word Works, Inc. Her poetry and fiction has appeared in a variety of reviews and anthologies. She is a recent PEN Syndicated Fiction winner.

MAXINE COMBS has published short fiction, poetry, and book reviews in many small press journals. A pamphlet of her poems, *Letters From Burning Buildings*, is scheduled to be published by the Nebraska Poetry Association. Her short story, "Plateglass Window," won the Larry Neal Fiction Award in Spring 1988. She lives and teaches in Washington, DC.

PETER COYNE teaches at Humboldt State University in the Speech Communication Department.

SALLY CROFT, a native of Massachusetts, has lived in northern California for the past twenty years. Her work appears in the current anthology *Deep Down* and in *Light Year '86*. She has also appeared in a number of small press publications, including *Seneca* and the *Bellingham Review*. At present she is working on an autobiographical novel *The House on Grant Street*. She teaches writing at San Jose State University.

BARBARA CROOKER lives with her husband and three children, the youngest of whom is autistic. She occasionally teaches creative writing at Cedar Crest College, gardens, plays tennis, and cross-country skis. Over 300 of her poems have been published in journals, anthologies, and in six books. Her awards include a Fellowship in Literature from the Pennsylvania Council on the Arts and a prize in the NEA/*Passages North* Emerging Writers Competition.

PENELOPE DEAKIN, a grape farmer, is a learning center director and journalism instructor at State University of New York, College at Fredonia, and a college newspaper adviser. She's been writing poetry for fourteen years and has published in anthologies and small magazines, including an anthology of New York State poets, *On Turtles Back* (White Pine Press), and the anthology *From Seed Bed to Harvest* (Seven Buffalos Press).

MARK DEFOE lives in Buckhannon, West Virginia, where he is chairperson of the English department at West Virginia Wesleyan College. He has published his work widely in the US, Canada and Europe. His two books of poetry are *Bringing Home Breakfast* (Black Willow), and *Palmate* (Pringle Tree Press). His poetry has appeared in *Yale Review, North American Review, Kenyon Review, Paris Review*, and others.

EMILIO DE GRAZIA's poems have been published in several journals although he has made his mark mainly as a writer of short fiction. His collection, *Enemy Country* (New Rivers, 1984) was selected as a Writer's Choice, and though he is currently working on longer fiction, he wants to be a poet when he grows up.

PAMELA DITCHOFF's poetry has been published in *Amelia*, 1988: winner of the Bernice Jennings Traditional Poetry Competition, *The South Coast Poetry Review*, 1986, *Borderland*

(Artsite Press, Canada, 1986), and *This Year's Venison* (Sonora Review, 1983). Currently enrolled in the Ph.D. program at Michigan State University, she teaches poetry writing as a graduate assistant. She also teaches poetry writing to gifted elementary and secondary students and has recently completed a textbook on this subject.

NANCY DU PLESSIS is a poet and journalist who specializes in stage solo performances of her own work. American born, she is based in New York and Paris. Her publications include a collection of poems, *BUD*, and a forthcoming collection *Bleak House/Partly Sunny Skies*.

ELIZABETH EDDY was born in East Cleveland. She is a lifetime professional painter and print maker, exhibiting her work throughout the US since 1930. Poetry publications began in 1976 and include *litany*, a chapbook, (Coffee House Press 1984), *Contemporary Education* (University of Indiana, 1987), *Light Year '87*, humorous verse, (Case Western Reserve University), *Rambunctious Review*, 1987. Her first book of poems will be published in Spring, 1989.

W.D. EHRHART teaches at Germantown Friends School in Philadelphia where he lives with his wife Anne and two-year-old daughter, Leela. His most recent collection of poems is *Winter Bells* (Adastra Press, 1988).

SUE SANIEL ELKIND was born in Pittsburgh where she has remained all of her life. She began writing poetry at the age of sixty-four. She founded the Squirrel Hill Poetry Workshop under the sponsorship of the Carnegie Library. She has published four poetry collections: *No Longer Afraid* (Lintel, 1985), *Waiting for Order* (Naked Man Press, 1988), *Dinosaurs and Grandparents* (MAF Press, 1988), and *Another Language* (Papier-Mache' Press, 1988). Her work has appeared in over 150 magazines and reviews. She was a recipient of the 1987 Esther Scheffler Poetry Award of Michigan State University.

AISHA ESHE is widely published throughout the country. Her poetry has appeared in *Sing Heavenly Muse, Black American Literature Forum, Helicon Nine*, and *Heresies*. A novella, *Blood at the Root*, will be published Spring 1989 by Esoterica Press, Barstow, California.

RINA FERRARELLI came to the US from Italy at fifteen. She teaches English part-time at the University of Pittsburgh and is the mother of a daughter and two sons. She has original poems in recent issues of *La Bella Figura, Kansas Quarterly, Laurel Review*, and *The McGuffin*. A chapbook of translations was recently published by *Mid-American Review*. She has just received the Italo Calvino Prize from the Columbia Translation Center for *Light Without Motion*, forthcoming from Owl Creek Press.

ELIZABETH FOLLIN-JONES writes poetry, short stores, and essays. Her poetry has appeared in various journals, her essays in *The Washington Post* and *The Christian Science Monitor*. She won third prize, 1986 Judith Siegel Pearson Award for a poetry manuscript. One of her short stories was selected by the 1987 Pen Syndicated Fiction Project. She is a graduate of the University of Michigan.

NANCY BENGIS FRIEDMAN: Since arriving in NYC in 1978 I've gained an MA (Columbia Univ.), a husband and two sons. The latter have done more than anything else to inspire metaphor. To release that creative energy I am teaching and writing. My work has appeared in *Lips, Amelia, eleven*, and *Up Against the Wall, Mother*. I've also discovered a new field: poetry therapy, right now working with senior citizens.

ALICE BLOOM FUCHS enjoyed single parenting of four children for a number of years. She then married and moved out of the suburbs to start farming. She is working on a poetry chapbook and a novel and will begin teaching at the University of Pittsburgh this fall where she will receive her Master in Writing. Her poetry has appeared in *Plainswoman, Sojourner, Lapis, Sunrust* and others. She attends the Women's Creative Writing Workshop at Carlow College.

PATRICIA GARFINKEL's poems have been published in *Visions, Seattle Review, Hollins Critic,* and in many other magazines. Her work has also appeared in numerous anthologies. A chapbook, *Ram's Horn,* was published in 1980 by Window Press. Her work has also been translated into Korean. She lives in Reston, Virginia, and works full time as a speech writer in the U.S. House of Representatives.

MICHAEL S. GLASER, the father of five children, teaches literature and creative writing at St. Mary's College of Maryland where he also directs the annual Festival of Poets and Poetry. He is a Poet-in-the-Schools for the Maryland Arts Council. He is editor of *The Cooke Book: A Seasoning of Poets* (SCOP Publications, 1987) and recently published a broadside of his poems, "On Being A Father" (Seasonings Press). A collection of his work is forthcoming from The Bunny and Crocodile Press.

BARBARA GOLDBERG is a recipient of Fellowships from the NEA, Corporation of Yaddo, Individual Artist's grant from Maryland State Arts Council, Columbia University Translation Center Award, and twice winner of PEN Syndicated Fiction Project Competition. Her work has appeared in *Poetry, American Scholar, Antioch Review, NER/BLQ,* and elsewhere. She is the author of *Berta Broadfoot and Pepin the Short: A Merovingian Romance* (The Word Works and simultaneously in Canada by The Porcupine's Quill).

BINA GOLDFIELD lives and works in New York City. She is the winner of the 1988 Hans S. Bodenheimer Award, Andrew Mountain Press. She has been published in *Slant, Bitterroot,* and *Thirteen* and has self-published a feminist handbook, *The Efemcipated English Handbook* (Westoner Press).

MARION GOLDSTEIN works as a poetry therapist at a private psychiatric hospital in New Jersey. She has published articles on poetry therapy in *The Arts in Psychotherapy* and *The Journal of Social Psychology*. Her poetry has been published by *Caesura, Stone Country,* and *The Christian Science Monitor.*

SANDRA GREGORY has recently begun to photograph her subjects in black and white. She particularly enjoys capturing the strength and dignity of her friends and family living in rural Texas areas.

URSULA HEGI is the author of a novel *Intrusions* (Viking) and a collection of short stories *Unearned Pleasures and Other Stories* (University of Idaho Press). Her fiction, poetry, and book reviews have appeared in the *New York Times, Poetry Northwest, Ms., Poetry,* and many other publications. Her awards include grants from the Washington State Arts Commission, PEN/NEA Fiction Project, Northwest Institute for Research, and Artist Trust.

GILBERT HONIGFELD is a mainstream contemporary poet, a product of public schools and a small state university campus downtown at the other end of the #7 bus line, where some of his best classes were held in a renovated brewery that smelled of wet mash on rainy days. Now, he is a frequent contributor to *Waterways, Slipstream,* and other literary magazines.

LOWELL JAEGER is a 1981 graduate of the Iowa Writer's Workshop and a 1986 recipient of an NEA Fellowship for Creative Writers. Recently he was awarded the 1987 Grolier Poetry Peace Prize. His first full-length collection of poems, *War On War,* is forthcoming from Utah State University Press.

JUDSON JEROME was born in Tulsa, Oklahoma, and took degrees from Ohio State University and the University of Chicago, afterwards embarking on a highly successful academic career, including a twenty year tenure at Antioch College. He was widely published with numerous books to his credit, ranging from poetry and verse drama to literary textbooks and criticism. He was well known for his monthly article on the craft of poetry. He died in 1991.

LOUISE M. KIRST-GESCH has lived in the Los Angeles South Bay area all her life. She is a graduate of California State University, Long Beach and the University of San Diego. She is currently an assistant to the Theatre Production Manager for the Center for the Arts program at El Camino College. Mother of two little girls, she loves to take pictures of her family doing anything and everything.

WILLA KORETZ, an emigré from New Jersey, began her career as writer in the Young Poets Program at Harvard in 1971. A dancer as well, she incorporates her poetry and essays into performances and workshops, travelling the United States to share her images in both words and the language of dance. She lives in Santa Fe, New Mexico, and her poetry is most recently included in *Rainbows & Rhapsodies-Poetry of the Eighties* by Fine Arts Press.

BARBARA LAU, a dual resident of Austin, Texas, and Decatur, Illinois, writes feature articles and non-fiction books for profit, and poetry and fiction for love. Her poems have appeared in *Spoon River Quarterly, The Alchemist,* and *Koroné.* She attended the Iowa Writer's Program last summer and hopes to finish her novel before her adopted baby arrives.

LYNN LAUBER was born and raised in Ohio and now lives in Rockland County, New York, where she earns her living as an editor and fiction abridger. Her stories have appeared in various literary magazines, including *Stories* and *Fiction Network.* Her collection of stories, *White Girls,* will be published by Norton in the fall of 1989.

REGINALD LOCKETT was born in Berkeley and grew up in West Oakland. He earned both a B.A. and M.A. in English Literature at San Francisco State University. He teaches at City College of San Francisco. Poems, reviews, and articles have appeared in almost three dozen anthologies and periodicals including *Iowa Review, A.C.T. Preview,* and *Quilt.* His first book of poetry, *Good Times & No Bread* was published in 1978 (Jukebox Press). *Where The Birds Sing Bass* will be published in 1989 by Blue Light Press.

GERALD LOCKLIN teaches English at California State University at Long Beach and has published over thirty-five volumes of poetry and fiction. Three books have appeared in translation in West Germany from Maro Verlag and Goldmann Verlag. His most recent collection of poems is *Children of a Lesser Demagogue* (Wormwood Review Press). A collection of short stories, *The Gold Rush*, will appear from Applezaba Press this winter.

ELLIE MAMBER has been published in the *Connecticut River Review, Beacon Review*, and in *Women and Aging* (Calyx). A lifelong resident of the Boston area, she is the mother of a son, happily married, and, to her delight, a grandmother as well. Her work involves developing and administering social service programs in her community.

ERNEST MARSHALL was born in Columbus, Ohio, but lived most of his life in the South. He presently teaches philosophy at East Carolina University in Greenville, North Carolina. He has been attempting to write poetry (intermittently) since college days, but in a serious way only within the last few years. He has published poems in *Roanoke Roots, A Carolina Literary Companion*, and *The Greensboro Review*.

RIC MASTEN was born in Carmel, California, in 1929. He has toured extensively over the last twenty-two years, reading his poetry in more than 400 colleges in North America, Canada, and England. He is a well-known conference theme speaker and is a regular on many television and radio talk shows. He lives with his wife Billie Barbara just south of Carmel in the Big Sur mountains. He has nine books to his credit.

MAUDE MEEHAN, wife, mother, teacher, student, editor, political person, in ever fluctuating order, has been widely published in literary journals, magazines, textbooks, and anthologies. Her book, *Chipping Bone*, published in 1986, is going into its third printing. She is a frequent guest lecturer in fields relating to women's studies and has been conducting writing workshops for women in Santa Cruz, California, for several years.

MARGIT MOORE's poems and short stories have appeared in *Seattle Review* and *Tidewater*. She is the mother of two young sons and the owner of a landscape design business in Kirkland, Washington. As a founding member of Laughing Woman Press, she has organized several public readings in the Greater Seattle Area, providing a new forum for the vivid voices of Northwest women poets.

JANICE TOWNLEY MOORE, a native of Atlanta, teaches English at Young Harris College in the mountains of North Georgia. Her poetry has appeared in over two dozen journals and anthologies, including *Southern Poetry Review, Kansas Quarterly, Anthology of Magazine Verse*, and *The Bedford Introduction to Literature*.

BONNIE MICHAEL PRATT is a freelance writer and poet living in Winston-Salem, North Carolina. Her special interests are women's issues and metaphysics. She has published in many literary magazines as well as commercial magazines and has been included in several anthologies.

LINDA QUINLAN, house painter and working class lesbian mother, writes short stories and poetry. She has appeared in the publications *Sinister Wisdom, Conditions, Fireweed,* and *The Poet.*

JOHN RENNER is an administrator at a school for students with learning disabilities. John's photographs often appear with Patti Tana's poetry. "Ask the Dreamer Where Night Begins" is a picture of Patti and their son Jesse.

ELISAVIETTA RITCHIE's poems, translations, articles, reviews, and photos have been published in the *New York Times, Washington Post, The Christian Science Monitor, New Republic,* and hundreds of other publications. She is the recipient of many awards, including three-time winner of the PEN/NEA Syndicated Fiction Project competitions for three of her stories, and one of these also won *Amelia* 1985 Reed Smith Fiction Prize. She is editor of *The Dolphin's Arc,* an anthology of poems on endangered marine species.

ROSE ROSBERG was a New York City high school librarian for many years. Her collection of poems, *Trips-Without LSD,* was published by Fiddlehead Poetry Books. Her poems have appeared in *Images, new renaissance, Poets On, Southern Poetry Review,* and other magazines and anthologies of verse.

TERESA NOELLE ROBERTS formerly lived in New York City where she was in public relations for publishing companies. She lives now outside of Ithaca on a dirt road that cuts through a gravel quarry. She freelances for the local "alternative weekly," writes poetry, and ploughs away on a novel that has, as a sub-plot, the reconciliation of an estranged father and daughter. Her work has appeared in *Sojourner, Bellowing Ark, Proofrock,* and *The Christian Science Monitor.*

NANCY FROST ROUSE has a B.A. in English, writes poetry, and short stories, and is currently co-authoring a book of fiction. Her poems have appeared in numerous publications and anthologies, including the *Weymouth* anthology of the N.C. Poetry Society.

SAVINA A. ROXAS writes poetry, fiction, and non-fiction. She holds an M.F.A. and Ph.D. from the University of Pittsburgh, and is formerly a Professor at Clarion State University. Her work has recently appeared in *Antagonish Review, Black Fly, Sunrust,* and *Modern Haiku.*

DEIDRE SCHERER is a visual artist who works in fabric and thread. For the past eight years she has focused on creating a special series of art pieces, *Images of Aging.* A resident of Williamsville, Vermont, she received her B.F.A. from the Rhode Island School of Design. She was selected as an Artist-in- Residence by the Vermont Council of the Arts in 1978. She has shown her work in numerous group and solo exhibitions and her sewn fabric heads were featured in a recent cover article of *Threads* magazine (Issue 16, April 88).

BETTIE SELLERS is a Goolsby Professor of English at Young Harris College, Georgia, and author of five collections of poetry, including *Spring Onions and Cornbread* and *Morning of the Red-Tailed Hawk*. She was given the Governor's Award for the Humanities in 1987 for work in preservation of Georgia's unique Literary Heritage. Her new collection, *Wild Ginger*, is due out in late 1988.

JOANNE SELTZER is the author of *Adirondack Lake Poems* (1985) and two new chapbooks, *Suburban Landscape* and *Inside Invisible Walls*. In addition to poetry she has published short fiction, literary essays, and translations of French poetry.

CATHERINE SHAW, of New York City, has written many poems about her father, the late Edward L. Shaw. In addition to family life, her major themes are the human body and the world of work. Her publication credits include *Poets on Outerbridge, Slant*, and the 10th Anniversary edition of *Kalliope*. She has written articles for national magazines and edited books for major publishers.

PHILLIP SHELTON was born in Oregon in 1945. Since 1964 he has lived and worked in Los Angeles as a jewelry manufacturer. Photography is his avocation and a diary of his times.

ENID SHOMER's poems and stories have appeared in *Poetry, Ploughshares, The Women's Review of Books, Apalachee Quarterly*, and many other magazines and anthologies. She is the author of two chapbooks and of *Stalking the Florida Panther*, winner of the poetry book prize of The Word Works in 1987. Among her other national awards are the *Writer's Digest* Writing Competition in Poetry, The Eve of St. Agnes Prize, and the Washington Prize.

ANITA SKEEN is currently an Associate Professor of English at Wichita State University in Wichita, Kansas, where she teaches in the M.F.A. Program in Creative Writing and in the Women's Studies Program. She is a member of the Board of Directors of the Kansas Committee for the Humanities and is active in the state's Artist-in-Education Programs. She has published in numerous literary magazines, including *Prairie Schooner, New Letters*, and *Nimrod*. She is the author of a volume of poems entitled *Each Hand A Map* (The Naiad Press).

FLOYD SKLOOT was born in Brooklyn and now lives in Portland, Oregon. He has published two chapbooks of poems, *Rough Edges* (Chowder Chapbooks, 1979) and *Kaleidoscope* (Silverfish Review Press, 1986). His poems have appeared in *Harper's, Shenandoah, New England Review/Bread Loaf Quarterly*, and *Prairie Schooner*. His daughter Rebecca is now sixteen.

LU V. SMITH has been writing for publication since the age of eight. Her poetry has won many awards and been widely published in college journals, small press, and national publications. Recent poems have appeared in *The Christian Science Monitor, Cats Magazine*, and the *Wisconsin Poets Calendar for 1989*. As a freelance writer, she also writes articles, short stories, and essays, but her first love was poetry and it remains her favorite means of communication for everything from humor to the day's social issues.

AMBER COVERDALE SUMRALL is co-editor of *In Celebration of the Muse, Writings by Santa Cruz Women*. She co-produces the reading series of the same name, now in its eighth season. Her work appears in *Negative Capability, Passages North, The Women's Review of Books*, and others. She lives in the Santa Cruz mountains.

PATTI TANA teaches at Nassau Community College, SUNY, and is on the editorial board of *Esprit: A Humanities Magazine*. She participated in the production and performance of an album of women's work songs, *The Work of the Women*, and is the author of two books of poetry, *How Odd This Ritual of Harmony* and *Ask the Dreamer Where Night Begins*.

RANDEANE TETU has received several national awards for fiction. A resident of Haddam, Connecticut, her work appears in *The Massachusetts Review, Loonfeather, The Fiddlehead*, and other magazines. She has written two collections of short stories and is currently working on her third novel.

BARBARA L. THOMAS is a Pacific Northwest poet and calligrapher. She has been most recently published in *Stone Country, Tide Water*, and *IYE: Audio-Visual Magazine*. She is one of the founders of Laughing Woman Press.

CINDA THOMPSON is a native of Southern Illinois, although she now lives in Peoria and works for a textbook publisher. Her poems were most recently published in *Rainbows and Rhapsodies* (Fine Arts Press, 1988). Prizes include first place for poetry, Bensalem Association of Women Writer, 1987, and placement as a poetry finalist *Iowa Woman*, 1988.

LORRAINE TOLLIVER is a native of Kentucky. She teaches in the English Department at West Los Angeles College. Her short stories and poems have appeared in *Poetry L/A, Writers International, Appalachian Heritage*, and *College Journal, LA*.

DONNA TRUSSELL grew up in Texas and now edits an entertainment magazine in Kansas City. She lives downtown with her husband, a songwriter and journalist. She loves bad taste, Judy Canova, and has seen *Glen or Glenda?* five times. She is a member of two writers' groups. Her work has appeared in *The Massachusetts Review, Poetry Northwest, American Fiction '88, Tar River Poetry*, and other journals.

BERYLE WILLIAMS is a book review editor and columnist for the *Minnesota Women's Press* and until Spring 1988 was poetry and fiction editor for *WARM Journal* in Minneapolis. A past recipient of a Minnesota State Arts Board Fellowship in poetry, her poems have appeared in numerous journals and anthologies, including *Milkweed Chronicle, Lake Street Review, The Poet Dreaming in the Artist's House* (Milkweed Editions), and *Border Crossings* (New Rivers Press).

LENORE WILSON has an M.A. in Creative Writing from the University of California, Davis. Her work has been published in such magazines as *The California Quarterly, Five Fingers Review, Berkeley Poetry Review*, and *Blue Unicorn*. She currently teaches creative writing at Napa Valley College.